Aerial 2009

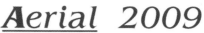

John Glenn's Fine Arts Magazine

"Beneath the Surface"

John Glenn High School

201 John Glenn Drive

Walkerton, Indiana 46574

Enrollment: 608

Volume 26

Photo and Cover Photos by Kayleigh McMichael, Senior

"We live amid surfaces, and the true art of life is to skate well on them."
- Ralph Waldo Emerson

To pass beneath the surface of a being is to begin to penetrate into the depths of complete meaning and understanding. The surface of that separate world, like a mirror, an appearance, provides one insight into the being whether it be a bluff or raw emotion. Writing and art represent a gateway of passing through that surface into true self-identity and self-reflection. Digest the works of our writers and artists as they dabble beneath the surface in ink and paint.

beneath the surface

AuthorHouse™
1663 Liberty Drive, Suite 200
Bloomington, IN 47403
www.authorhouse.com
Phone: 1-800-839-8640

First published by AuthorHouse 3/6/2009

ISBN: 978-1-4389-6439-3 (sc)

Printed in the United States of America
Bloomington, Indiana

This book is printed on acid-free paper.

Patrons

Platinum
DC Wellness

Joe and Bethany Laizure

Miller's Merry Manor

Tri Kappa, Epsilon Chi Chapter

Gold
Deacons of the Walkerton Presbyterian Church

Falcon 500 Club

John Small Insurance

Lee Back

Lewie and Eileen Reed

Teacher's Credit Union

The Minker Family

Silver
Klaudia Kovach

Graphic Literature

Bronze
Glenn Wisnieski, D.D.S.

Plastic Components

Tangles- Kelly Prentkowski

Boosters
Corner Cup Cafe

Eberly Orchard

1st Source Bank

Just For You

Kids' Korral Daycare

Lindsey Houston

Aerial Staff

editors Heather Helminger and Kayleigh McMichael

editorial staff April Allen, Ariel Beatty, Chloe Bugajski, Kaitlin Cassady, DaLynn Clingenpeel, Kelsey Dreessen, Michael Fansler, Amanda Foresman, Nathan Gardner, Kayla Goforth, Heather Helminger, Ethan Horvath, Lindsey Houston, Emily Jaske, Kate Jenkins, Breanna Kretchmer, Jacob Ladyga, Jordan Lynch, Kayleigh McMichael, Avalon Minker, Eva Paulsteiner, Josh Phillips, Cassie Philson, Kelsey Piotrowicz, Aaron Santana, Drew Vance, Patricia Weiss

design and layout Kayla Goforth, Heather Helminger, Kate Jenkins, Breanna Kretchmer, Jordan Lynch, Kayleigh McMichael, Josh Phillips, Kelsey Piotrowicz, Drew Vance, Patricia Weiss

art advisor Mr. John Thomas

***aerial* and literary advisor** Mr. Paul Hernandez

administration Superintendent Richard Reese
Principal William Morton
Assistant Principal Mark Maudlin

printers AuthorHouse
1663 Liberty Drive, Suite 200
Bloomington, Indiana 47403
Ryan McConnell, Book Consultant
Adalee (Pairitz) Cooney, Production Supervisor

"[Our] role in society, or any artist or poet's role, is to try and express what we all feel. Not to tell people how to feel. Not as a preacher, not as a leader, but as a **reflection** *of us all."*
- John Lennon, in an interview with KFRC RKO radio given on the day of his death, December 8, 1980 -

Contents

fiction

drama

prose

poetry

Contents

poetry cont'd.

art

Contents

Past Reflections

beneath the surface

"We spend most of our time and energy in a kind of horizontal thinking. We move along the surface of things [but] there are times when we stop. We sit still. We lose ourselves in a pile of leaves or its memory. We listen and breezes from a whole other world begin to whisper."

- James Carroll

Photo by Kayleigh McMichael, Senior

The Past slumbers beneath the covers of the present, just waiting to be shaken like the precious snow globes of childhood. Reflected in pictures from our youth, in precious keepsakes and momentos, just beneath the surface lies our youth and childhood, our dreams and lessons learned. Dip down and immerse yourself in **past reflections**.

Scrunchies

Prose by Nicole Noland, Senior *Scholastic Writing Award Silver Key Winner*

A scrunchy is not what most people would consider the height of fashion, especially not ones that are crocheted out of colored yarn, with enough hairspray dried on them to stand up on their own. My mother owned a drawer full of these scrunchies when I was little, one to match any outfit. She would pull her long hair up in them, twisting the elastic band around a dark ponytail, as she got ready to leave for her job. I used to lie on her bed and watch her put on her catering uniform, spray herself with perfume and kiss me goodbye. I never wanted her to leave; I wanted her to stay home and play Barbies with me. I never understood she had to work because we needed the money.

It wasn't until I was in high school that I realized she catered at the Jefferson Street houses in South Bend because it was something she could do at night, when my brother and I were asleep. She could be my mother during the day and a room mom to my first grade class. She could bring in cupcakes with Winnie the Pooh on them for my birthday and go to my Girl Scout meetings, but at night, she had to be an hors d'oeuvre server, walking around houses we could never afford, plastering a fake smile on her face as the spoiled trophy wives told her that "the help" was to use the basement bathroom and not the one in their homes. She did this night after night because she didn't want her children to be in daycare or have a babysitter because she had a day job.

Looking back, I almost feel guilty for the way I would act when she left. I would cry and hug her leg, begging her to stay home with me. She would pry me off and hand me to my dad, telling me she would be home when I woke up. Then, leaving a pink lipstick stain on my cheek, she would close the front door and drive off in her maroon minivan.

She was always right. I would forget about her as soon as my dad distracted me with his silly dinner creations and Southern rock albums. Looking at the scrunchies now, I'll sometimes smile and remember when he would make us Hamburger Helper, announcing that it was called Cat Soup Fillet. Beef and noodles turned into Weasel Snouts and Possum Feet. Chicken nuggets became Roadkill. When he would forget to name his creations, I would refuse to eat until he gave it a disgusting title. Sometimes the scrunchies remind me of going through his collection of record albums and picking out the ones with strange pictures on the front. We would jump around like maniacs, screaming for him to play his White Snake songs. It wasn't like we even knew who that was; we just thought we were cool because he would make the room vibrate with noise.

Inevitably, bedtime would come, and I would instantly want my mom. The scrunchies remind me of that, more than anything. I would lie in my bed and cry because I missed her and wanted her to tuck me into bed. Eventually, I would get up and tiptoe into the bathroom, opening her drawer of scrunchies. Picking one out, I would snap it on my wrist and sneak back into bed. Hiding under my covers, I would pull my arms around my face, breathing in the smell of her hairspray and shampoo. I'd fall asleep with my arms sprawled across my face, and she would wake me up when she got home.

Sometimes, I'll pull one of those scrunchies out of the drawer, now filled with my make-up and flat-irons. She doesn't wear them anymore; she hasn't since she cut off all of her hair. I'm always a little nervous someone will burst in, asking, "What are you DOING?" Then I decide I don't care, and sniff them away. I still get a little sad thinking about if I'm going to turn into that sad little girl again when I go away to college, wishing for her mommy. Who knows? Maybe I'll take a couple of scrunchies with me to sleep with.

My Picture of Pictures

Poetry by Doc Borlik, Senior
Photo Slip of a younger Doc and his father Robert

This slip of pictures
Has never left my bedroom
It is too dear to me
But over time, over years
Many changes it has seen
But it is not just the changes of my room
More than just new paint, furniture, and rearrangement
It has seen me change
Grow up over the years
These pictures are faded
But the memory is not
The memory is what is important
And the good times it brought
You see, I was five or six or seven
Back in the day when ugly sweaters were in style
My father and I were at the mall
To pick up a few things
While on our way out
There was a photo booth towards the exit
We both looked at each other
As the same thought ran through our minds
"Let's have some fun and get our photos!"
Just of father and son
So we paid up our dues and read the instructions
Decided what to do and hit the button
I remember his exact words still to this day
"Let's take one normal one then we can be silly and play"
The camera counted us down
I smiled with such glee
Despite my crooked smile
I was happy as could be
The booth lit up, a flash
Now came the fun
I thought for a quick second
And did a face as funny as I could imagine
My dad kept his smile
Until I finally told him to do something fun
Now there's that one tiny square
Of silly father and son
To this day, I hold that picture deep
That is one memory I plan to keep

A Little Song and Dance

Prose by April Allen, Senior
Pencil by Kate Smith, Junior

> *" I danced in and out, off the ground like a reflection from glass gliding against the walls."*

Running through my old, gray house, singing at the top of my lungs, Peter Pan was stuck in my head. I always believed I was Tiger Lily and that I could dance like her. I never gave a care in the world who would watch me or who was listening. I never cared if I could sing or dance exceptionally well at all. I stayed in my own little world of primary colors and sunny skies. The rain couldn't make my day blue because I'd still be in that happy place, dancing in the rain, singing in the rain. Mom had the video recorder taping my every move; I didn't care who was watching. I sang my little heart out. I danced till my feet were numb. "You silly monkey, you," my mom would always say. I'd be there twirling, leaping, yodeling and maybe even singing a bit too loud. I didn't care. I danced in and out, off the ground like a reflection from glass gliding against the walls.

I'm still that girl. Although I may have a rough exterior, my interior is quite fragile, like glass. I can be in my room for hours singing and dancing like nobody's watching, like nobody can hear or see me. That's also how I am on stage, pretending like nobody's there when I'm sharing my gift, doing the thing I love most.

I Grew Up

Poetry by Emily Enders, Senior
Watercolor by Kayleigh McMichael, Senior

I grew up with bright eyes
And a wandering imagination,
Escaping into a separate world,
Into a never ending pasture of overgrown tulips
And snapdragons that came to life
Practically animatronic
But completely soulful,
All while in the comfort of Grandma's front yard,
Hearing bedtime stories that swept me back in
To the world that knew only me.
I grew up.
Years later I walk through the same garden
As the reincarnated flowers
That once amused me
With their antics and played in my little world
Are now stifled.
I gaze into their centers and remember
The fun I had
When I was growing up.

Lavon: Before

*Poetry by Alyssa Wiegand, Senior
Photo of Alyssa's Grandmother
Lavon Nickles*

Look at her,
my favorite picture of a happy, older lady,
smiling, her face lit up,
false teeth showing a slight glint in the light.
This is my grandmother,
the one I know the best,
but also the one who is getting harder to remember
with each passing year.
I don't remember her smiling like this
nearly as much as I remember
her pain and suffering.
Looking at her photo,
people often see a grandmother,
a mother, a wife,
hair dyed light brown, golden rimmed glasses,
and her usual lipstick.
When I look at the photo,
it reminds me that there were happy times
before the months' long hospital stays,
before dialysis,
before the pain even morphine couldn't numb.
Long before she forgot who we were,
her memories bogged down in a drug induced haze,
drugs that only prolonged the inevitable.
Despite all of that,
I'm glad we have the photo.
See, this is probably one of the few pictures
I have of her as I choose to remember her.
My grandma was my world
long before I knew what the world was.
I'm glad I have a way to remember
her beautiful smile.
This picture has helped us all to heal;
to see her smile again
helped us all to smile.

[Beneath the Surface]   13

That Picture

Prose by Colten deFluiter, Senior
The Photo of Matt Morris and Colten deFluiter

As I am in my room packing for a long trip to Mexico and zipping up my suitcase, I almost forget my pictures. I go to my top drawer and pull out my only picture album. One picture catches my eye...

A picture is a moment frozen in time, and when someone decides to freeze that space and time, it can become much more. My picture is not like those new digital photos. There is no computer file with this one. Some pictures are significant to the whole world, like the ones from Pearl Harbor or a man landing on the moon. Most are only important to a few people. For example, my special photo would be "just another picture" to anyone else. But this is the only picture I have of my friend Matt Morris and me.

I will never forget how this picture came to me. I was sitting in the school lunchroom two weeks after his death, in my own little world full of sadness and loathing of the memories of the funeral, when Mrs. Rider gently tapped me on the shoulder and face down handed me the picture. I glanced at it and then put it away; I instantly recognized it from the yearbook. It would be a day or so before I could look at it, and a week before I could look at it without crying. This picture was more than just a moment in time. It was a reminder of the good times we had, the good times that were often overshadowed by his untimely death.

My photo is of my friend and me. It is taken at lunch during my 9th grade year. It shows the lunchroom with kids caught in their day to day conversation. At the top of the picture, there is a small rip, and the corners are bent from my two years of carrying it around. It shows us striking a manly, seductive poise.

To me, my picture looks like a window to a specific time and place; a window, a bit tattered and torn by some unknown storm. Everyday I wish I could climb through this window to a simpler time, before all the harshness of the real world and the reality of my own and everyone else's mortality surfaced around me. A time when all I had to worry about was what to wear for the next Homecoming day.

As I put the picture back into my picture album, I think of how much I've changed and will continue to change in the years to come. Yet there will always be that picture, that moment that will never change in my heart and mind.

Time to Fly Away

Prose by Conrad Schubert, Senior
Pencil by Mariah Rippy, Freshman

"I know it hurts to say goodbye, but it's time for me to fly." When most people think of family they don't include extended family. They may include cousins, aunts, and uncles. When I think of family, it's not just immediate family. It's the aunts and uncles, but it's also second and third cousins. It's the great uncles and great aunts. So when my family's turning point occurred, it had an impact on a large number of people.

With such a large family, it's pretty easy to have an impact on someone else. That's exactly what my cousin did, but he didn't have an impact on just one person. It was really the entire family. That's why when the incident occurred, it impacted many people.

When someone dies, he or she is usually remembered as being happy and always making people laugh. My cousin Isaac was no different. He always had a way of lightening the mood and easing the tension. He had his own entrance everywhere he went. At family gatherings he would always yell with his arms raised in the air, "My people!" It was his way of letting everyone know that he, "the party," had arrived, and the family would agree it had.

Isaac was known as the "haoka" of the family. A haoka can be defined pretty much as being backwards from everyone else, the goof ball, the one who has a different way of doing things. On a trip to Nebraska, I realized it was the perfect description for him. I spent a week with him on our trip to the Sundance. We spent every day together. We went golfing, rode horses, and slept in the same tent. He always had his own way of doing things.

No one has a real explanation for Isaac's suicide. A lot of people have their own reasons, but none are truly justified. I think it's just their way of dealing with his death. Personally, I've gone back and forth in different directions on how I feel about it. I've been confused. I've blamed other family members. And now, I think I'm getting over the stage of blaming Isaac. My explanation is he was the "haoka." His suicide was his backwards way of doing life. It was his own way of dying and it was on his terms. It may not be the actual reason, but I think it's the most reasonable.

For awhile, Isaac's death drove my family apart. Family gatherings weren't the same, and not everyone was coming to them. Recently, things are just getting back to normal, maybe even better. It may have even been Isaac's way of getting the family to be closer than before. When I think of Isaac, the words to that song come to mind, and despite the hurt, I believe it was just his time to fly.

Realistic Answers
to
Unrealistic Questions

Poetry by Kate Jenkins, Junior

Name:

It became me... or I became it soon after being asked, "Isn't Kate short for something...?" and shaking my head defiantly.

Date of Birth:

White. The kind of snow that has just fallen, without impurities, brand new, optimistic... analogous to the concept of birth. That day probably "smelled a lot like teen spirit"...or seldom washed flannel shirts.

Describe your early education:

How early? Still dark outside, the smell of sizzling bacon, hitting the snooze button once again. I learned the ways of respect after jumping farther off the swings than any boy. Ever since early, my knowledge has been less tangible, more prone to unraveling.

List your Awards and Honors:

- Being repeatedly let down...but somehow still believing as Anne Frank said, "All people are really good at heart."
- Surviving my first job (The smell of popcorn will forever remind me of the proper way to count back change; the pull of my neck as I strain to catch a glimpse of the clock... the minute hand in the same position as it has always been.)
- Feeling failure, but knowing it's not the end...Yes, a college will still accept you if you have an "A-"in gym.

Give a brief statement of your plans:

To know more... to experience it all. I want to feel the roar of the crowd at Fenway Park during yet another addition to the Red Sox vs. Yankees saga. I want to drive fifteen minutes from my home... and never see a corn field. But most of all... I want to be passionate about one thing...One thing to wake me up... One thing to keep me awake...One thing to make me feel that life is more than a series of random coincidences.

Quantitative Components

Poetry by Jacob Ladyga, Senior
Photo by Nekodah Niedbalski, Senior

1. Where were you born?
   On a pinhead of infinity dubbed 'Earth' by its English-speaking inhabitants.

2. Gender: M   F
   This simplistic dualism is inapplicable to a being of eternity.

3. Ethnicity?
   A Child of the Earth; the Air is my Breath, and the Waters, my Circulation.

4. Religion?
   Humanism: A Philosophy without Dogma. People are People- Love is our only Precept.

5. Hair Color?
   Dishwater blond hair, with light browns and highlights in hay-colored hues

6. Eye Color?
   The comparisons have been an Ocean and Chemical Spill. Look for Yourself.

7. Corporate Skills?
   None. My talents are natural and developed as such. I have no Passion for Business and its taxing Complications.

8. Address?
   Souls have no definitive physical residence. I am 'here' and 'there' only according to the limitations of description.

9. Former Employment?
   I am unsure of my full extent. One could argue vast experiences, should reincarnation be verified through the skeptics' sciences.

10. Social Security Number?
   155-47-7873 since   ALL-IS-PURE

Majority

Poetry by Kayla Goforth,
Junior
Pen by Nekodah Niedbalski,
Senior

I am fluffy and white.
I can change to many different colors,
white, gray, black, and even blue.
My colors show my emotion.
I am cloud.

I move constantly
As I visit different parts of the world.
I reflect what I see.
California, United States: Fires and dark clouds I am.
Iraq: Hot and windy with dark days ahead.
China: Hazy and less clear, as the smog covers everything.
Australia: Sunny, clear, white, fluffy cloud days.
Switzerland: Blinding white produces cold, chilly winds with snow.

When they're mad,
I'm mad, like the roadside bombs in Baghdad.
I reflect black with thunder and lighting.

When they're happy,
I'm happy, like the peace of the Berlin Wall's final collapse.
I reflect bright blue and white.

When they're sad,
I'm sad, like the hurricanes in the Gulf.
I reflect gray and windy, black rain.

Not everyone is the same;
Majority rules.
I reflect majority.

Fly Away

Poetry by Josh Phillips, Senior
Oil by Nicole Noland, Senior

Spread your wings, flying over frozen mountains,
Crystal rivers and geyser fountains,
Drifting above China's mystic forests.
Float with the breeze across seas to shore,
Deserts, cactus, and tumbleweeds,
Irish meadows, and fields of green.

Glide through cities of brick and stone,
Broken arenas of ancient Rome,
Haunted woodlands, forbidden trails,
Dust devils, caves, and OK Corrals,

Through castle halls, under waterfalls.
Pyramids crumble when nature calls,
Sky where blue becomes black with stars,
And lightning bugs are kept within jars.

Sand moves quickly through the hour glass.
Wings spread, we can all fly at last,
Rock will melt, coal crystallize,
Clouds with skylines materialize.
Spread wings and take flights over northern lights,
While wolves howl over blood red moonlit nights.

Kings and queens crown our dreams
As the sky rains diamonds and ruby things.
Oceans, rivers, lakes, and ponds,
Muslims travel to the lands of Koran.
Atlantis, hidden deep under forever,
Or golden tombs of pharaoh kings wrapped and
tethered.
Human voices cry out,
Echoes carry,
As angels dance with the cryptic fairies.
Gates of afterlife open swiftly.
Stay if you wish, or come fly with me.

My Little LEGO MAN

Prose by Don Hathaway, Senior

I was attending Bald Eagle Wilderness Boys Camp School, a boy's correctional camp founded by a Mennonite family to help troubled children. I had been sent there by my mother at the age of 11 to try and "fix" the problems that we had all the time. I was there for a year and a half. Over that year and a half, I met a lot of boys, and some of the ones that I met left before me. One of these boys had a family who lived at the end of the mountain on which the camp was located. His name was Dominic, and he was one of the best childhood friends I ever had. I remember the day he left. It was a sad day for me because I thought I would never see him again. We left each other with the usual parting; he gave me his address, I gave him mine, and we promised to write each other no matter what. My mind didn't comprehend how close to the camp his home actually was, and being that he was Mennonite in faith, he was very close to the camp counselors.

It was about five or six months after he left that Chief Crit, the head counselor at my campsite, announced we were all invited over to Dominic's house by his mother for dinner and for some fun and games. I couldn't have been any more excited. We walked to his house, which took a whole five minutes, and this let me know how

Photo of Don Hathaway's Original Lego Man

close he really was. I remember that we played a few games of Trees. That was the usual game for camp. I would explain, but that would take a whole page. By then it had gotten dark, so we went inside to eat. After we ate, all of us boys were just hanging out with the family in the living room. We weren't supposed to go anywhere else but the living room, but Dominic told me that he had something to give me in his bedroom. Being the kid that I was, I was excited because I was getting a present. When we got into the room, he gave me a little Lego man. I remember feeling…well…disappointed. My present was worth at the most one dollar, but then we started playing with his Legos. I remember getting in trouble because we were gone for about thirty minutes before they realized we were gone, and then they had to find us.

When we were about to leave, Chief Crit asked me if Dominic gave me anything, and I told him that he didn't. I remember feeling badly about lying because that was my first "major" lie; I was breaking a rule that was pretty big. When

> "In essence, that little **Lego** man represents my **entire childhood** because I never really had a childhood..."

to get the feel of being home again. One day as I was playing with my Legos, I found that little man. I remember sitting there and thinking about how long it had been since I had been at camp, and how much I liked it better then my own house at the time. Since then I have moved to three different children placement centers and five different foster homes. And yet, throughout all that chaos in my life, that little Lego man has stayed with me. He has been the perfect friend, in a sense, always there no matter what happens in my life. He is now in a cigar box that I got from my foster dad, along with other intrinsic objects.

When I look at him now, I remember the days when I didn't have to worry about the world, when the only thing that mattered in life was what game to play and where to play it. It reminds me of a whole year and a half of my life, spent in the mountains of Pennsylvania with a group of guys, doing nothing but playing around and having fun. It reminds me of little pow-wows that we had every night before we went to bed, of times spent running down the mountain side playing cowboys and Indians, of us standing by

we got back to the campsite, I put that little Lego man into my personal box, which was a wooden box that we used to keep personal items such as toothpaste, our Bible, combs, knives, and articles like that. I didn't know at the time that the Chiefs checked the boxes while we weren't there. Chief Crit came to me later that night and asked me if I had a toy in my personal box. Not knowing that he had checked in my box, I told him that I didn't. When he told me that he had checked it, I remember getting very mad at him for the first time ever, because I viewed that as an invasion of privacy. He took the toy and kept it for three months.

When I went on my first home visit, I took the toy back home and put it in a box full of my Legos. When I finally got home for good after a year and a half, I started going through all my things

the creek watching our hand carved boats race down the creek, of swimming in the Scootach River in the middle of winter with no shirt on and the water's temperature well below freezing as we had to break ice even to swim. It reminds me of times spent just looking at the stars, of canoe trips that lasted for three weeks straight, of fishing, of mud football, and so many other fond memories.

In essence, that little Lego man represents my entire childhood because I never really had a childhood at my old house or even at my new one. Life had a way of making me grow up too quickly, but that year and a half was the best time I have ever had. It was a time that was uninterrupted by anything bad, just us boys and the outdoors. It is amazing that such a small, "worthless" object can evoke such feelings in oneself. And that is the story of my little Lego man.

Runaway

Prose by Emily Jaske, Junior
Pencil by Allison Adkins, Junior

When I was four years old, I decided to go on an adventure. Wearing my favorite apple dress with the purple stain on it, I got out my little brother's stroller. I remember the handles being warm. Locating my cat that had no name, I placed her in the stroller and buckled her in so that she would be safe. I then started to push her down the gravel road. The cat didn't like being in the stroller; she was flipping all around. I remember seeing her black foot shoot up into the air like she was raising her hand in class, and it made me laugh. It was such a free feeling out in the open road, in control, the sun beating down on my face and the cat making me laugh so hard. I was traveling, walking No Name down to my neighbor's house who was Amish.

I was halfway there when my mom came out. She started to call my name. The look on her face was scared, relieved and angry. I hated that look on her face. I ran because it scared me, and I didn't want my freedom to be taken away. The feeling of being free was slipping away. Suddenly, the sun didn't feel right, and the open gravel road hurt my feet; it was all wrong. So I went back, promising myself I would continue that adventure. Now twelve years later, I still want to be that free again. I want to be able to run away, to travel without ever being stopped.

3 x 5

Poetry by Avalon Minker, Senior
Oil by Brooke Poeppel, Senior

I cannot see myself
I try so hard
I look into a mirror
She is not there
She is long, long gone
I feel the fear
That I have lost myself
Lost for good
Then I look on my dresser
There on a 3x5
I see myself
Tears in my eyes I reach for it
I pick it up and clutch it to my chest
I found myself I really did
I found it finally
She is so young, I am so old
She is my hope, my long lost self
I will never lose her again
I wish to place her so strongly
Beneath my wing
I wish to help so much
I cannot help
I cannot help at all
She is me and I am her
And yet the past is so long gone

Mirror Reflection

Poetry by Jessica Thacker, Senior

Today I saw it, I saw who I am,
My reflection staring beady-eyed back at me.
Oh ma'am, who are you?
Your face is sunken in, you have black rings
Hanging under your eyelids like a death sentence.
Your hair is matted torn and ripped
And you're bruised and beaten like a rotten apple,
Like my soul deep within.
Thoughts ooze out of my head
Like mud squishing through my toes.
These hands want to grasp the ghastly figure before me.
Where is the young girl I once knew?
Why aren't her bright green eyes
Glowing anymore? Her smile is faded,
Now just a frown.
The little girl I once knew is
Kidnapped, hidden deep inside,
Never allowed outside.

Today
I realized no longer will I hide.
It's time to let out what's been slumbering deep
Within and show the world that
Little girl who's been longing to come
Outside.

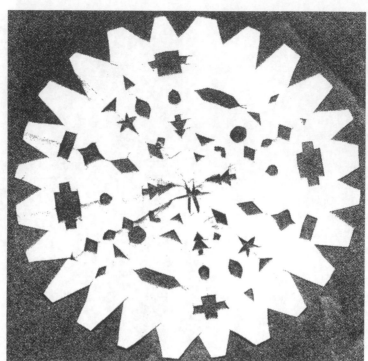

Life~and~Snow

Prose by Ashley Gilbert, Senior
Snowflake Cutout by Allison Adkins, Junior

I've always known that beauty is in the eye of the beholder. However, what happens when the beholder isn't a person, when the object of beauty is just that: an object? Something as soft, sweet, and delicate as falling snow doesn't have the ability to think it's beautiful. Instead, a person sees its beauty for it.

When I see snow falling, I can stare at the beauty of it for hours. To me, snow symbolizes growing up in the same way human life does. After it falls (symbolizing a child being born), I think it's the most beautiful thing in the world. Like a newborn child, there are no flaws to it while it just lies there, perfect and amazing. As the days go on, one can start to see footsteps in the snow, like the footsteps in a person's life. It's said that some people come in and out of your life and leave their footprints behind, which is true. While the footprints keep getting made, the snow that was once so perfectly laid out and put together starts to get messy. People's lives aren't scripted; they're lived in. A part of life is having a mess and dealing with it. This builds character and prepares for beauty to take over yet again. And finally many days after the snow falls, it begins to melt, yet leaves behind a trace of its existence, nourishing the earth it left behind, just like the end of a person's life and the influences each person leaves.

You can call me crazy, because I might be. I'm not sure why I can look at a sensational snowfall and see the symbolism between it and how my life was and/or will be. It's amazing to think that something so commonplace in nature can be connected with something that actually matters: life and existence. From all this, I can say that I've come up with something important to how I live my life. When my life ends, it will be like the melting of the snow. Something I can always remember is that lesson of the snow: after one snowfall melts, another snowfall just as beautiful and just as significant, always follows.

Seasons

Poetry by Phil VanWanzeele, Senior

Winter

Pure white landscapes mark the edges of the front and back of the earth.
The fields stand still like blank sheets of paper
Waiting for spring to bring on the paintbrush.
Old Man Winter exhales from his frigid cave mouth, blowing snow like hails of gunfire
Although softer and less violent.
It's so cold, you can see the pulsating veins of icicles.
Watch as white fades to green.

Spring

Green grass pokes through the snow like a cheese grater.
With each shedding smile, the sun sends Old Man Winter a farewell card.
The sky will cry a thousand times, sacrificing self dignity for the beauty of others.
Blooming flowers kiss the breeze, warmed by the soil.
It's so warm, the oak tree sheds off her sweater.
Watch as green fades to greener.

Summer

Water grabs each grain of sand by the hand and pulls them
In close for a lesson in rip currents
Every living creature so vibrant, so full of life,
Even the brick sidewalk seems to glow a little harder under the pounding of our feet.
Walk hand in hand to our lesson on rip currents;
Hurry before the Atlantic marks us tardy.
Watch as greener fades to orange.

Fall

The flowing green trees fade to orange as they kiss the summer sun goodbye.
Under gray skies the leaves sway loose, falling softly on the cold damp grass.
The softening sun slipping a little earlier each day reminds me
Old Man Winter will soon awake from his nap.
The swift wind bites as Old Man Winter's thunderous alarm clock roars.
Orange fades to white again.

Playing the bass

Prose by Aaron Rowe, Senior

Watercolor by Ashley Bloss, Senior

After a long day at school and being enthralled by music, I walked down the stairs of my basement to listen to my music. After plugging in my iPod and selecting the song "Whipping Post" by The Allman Brothers Band, I realized that I wanted to play along with it. So I went and got the one bass that I enjoy the most. As I opened up the case, I saw this magnificent piece of craftsmanship. Sunny is her name. I picked her up and placed her around my shoulders, admiring the "feel" of her.

My bass is an incredible piece of amazingness. There are two essential parts to my bass: the neck and the body. Both are made of wood. The neck, or fretboard as it is more commonly called, is made of brownish colored redwood. The body is sunburst colored, meaning that there is a black trim around the edge, and it's a mixture of orange and brown in the center. There is a whitish/manila pick guard surrounding the pickup. A bass has four metal strings that are thicker than guitar strings. It is heavier than a guitar and is longer and fatter, too. Basically, if Jesus returned and picked up an instrument, he'd play my bass.

What is a bass? A bass is a low pitched instrument for enjoyment or pleasure for your ears. It's the "thumping" instrument. A bass originated from the upright bass and the acoustic guitar. In the 1950's, Fender was one of the first to design the bass guitar. A bass has four strings, while a guitar has six strings. It has a similar body type, depending on what brand or style, and has the same electronics, despite the pickups. A bass is made of wood and/or metal, and keeps the low end and rhythm.

The bass is an awesome instrument. It symbolizes god in the way that it is the supreme ruling instrument. My bass is a vintage bass, which means it's old. Its age symbolizes experience. It was old and used when I got it. The edge of the body trim is black. The trim represents the dark times in my life. The center is bright orange. That represents the good times and my joy in playing. The size of my bass represents the awesomeness of it. It's bigger and better than a guitar. The tone of it is unbeatable. I've never played a bass of equal or better tone. It symbolizes who I am and what my lifestyle is.

I remember the day I got my bass. But before that happened, I had a doctor's appointment at Dr. Dieter's foot clinic. After I was finished, my dad and I went into his office, and he had this shiny, red Fender Jazz Bass. It was awesome. I said, "Wow, that's a cool guitar." That's when he told me it was a bass. I had to go back a week later for a routine checkup, and he had this old, vintage Fender Precision Bass. It was shiny sunburst colored. He sold it to me for $500. I also got a case with it. After that we went to a local music store and got a 20 watt Johnson amp. When we got home, I plugged her in and let it rip. I wasn't that good.

A week after I got my bass, I started taking lessons from an amazing teacher named Matt Girres. He later became a good friend and mentor, as well as my teacher. I played my vintage bass for hours. I'll never forget when I learned some of the hardest songs…by ear. That is extremely difficult for some people. The first hard song I learned was "I'm Your Captain" by Grand Funk Railroad. It starts with the guitar, but then leads to a riveting bass line. Later on, it's

followed by a bass solo. My bass is my money maker. It's led to a band with Adam and Sam, and numerous "gigs." It's my favorite thing in the world, and my sweet "Sunny" is my passion. I'll never forget that doctor's visit and the day that changed my life.

A Night at Grandma's

Prose by Michelle Clark, Senior

Pencil by Elizabeth Bella, Senior

A night at Grandma and Grandpa's house was like a vacation when my sister and I were younger. The minute we stepped in the door, Grandma wanted to know what we wanted for dinner, which was usually cut up bologna dipped in ketchup or mustard. After dinner, Grandma would have Melissa and I take a bath. Her bathtub, before she had the entire bathroom redone, had sliding glass doors and blue flowers that felt like sandpaper on our bare bottoms. When Grandma opened those precious sliding glass doors, my sister and I were forced to return from our fantasyland with our bath toys to dry off.

After Grandma dried us off and baby powered our freshly sanded behinds, we chose to dress up in her high fashion nightgowns. Melissa usually stole the silky green one from me, and I got the second-hand pink ensemble. However, I easily got over the situation because the time had come to do Grandma's make-up. She had a cabinet in the bathroom above the toilet that, on the first shelf, held her brushes and combs. On the second shelf was a gold mine. It was there we could find the infamous, 80's blue eye shadow, foundation powder, and maroon lipstick that was applied with a brush. To say the least, our grandma was the hippest on the block after we were done painting her face and attaching pink rollers to her weekly done up hair.

After the salon session, it was nearly our bedtime. For some reason, my grandma used to have two twin beds in her room. Melissa got the shorter, more comfortable bed, and I got the taller, hard as a rock bed that had attachable rails so that one didn't fall off. When we woke up in the morning, Grandma would usually make her famous French toast. Somehow, she found a way to make the perfect sweet-salty combination with crunchy edges. And if Grandma didn't fulfill our desires, Grandpa would return home from his daily walk uptown with a dozen or so donuts in tow.

Years have passed since those adventurous nights at Grandma and Grandpa's house. They have completely redone the bathroom, and Grandma got herself a new, queen-sized bed. However, some things remain steadfast. Grandma still makes the perfect French toast, and Grandpa faithfully makes his daily trip uptown.

ADDRESSING
MYSELF

What's your name?
Like a crisp morning with the frost on the grass
in the middle of the month in Spring.

Where do you live?
Off the borderline from a place where kids are
roaming the halls and adults sit impatiently
at their desks.

What color are your eyes?
They're the ocean waves that reflect off
the clover in the Irish hills of the unknown.

Who are you?
With big dreams in mind, a golden heart
inside, crazy all year round and a little rough
on the edges.

Are you married?
Have been for many centuries without any
knowledge of knowing that he was in my life
before I was even a sparkle in my mother's eye.

What do you symbolize?
The very essence of tranquility and prosperity
in love's eyes and a hint of insanity.

How do you feel right now?
Fireworks are shooting off, my heart is beating
five times faster than usual. I'm in love.

What are your goals?
A click of the button and off goes the flash
highlighting every concave and convex
of the world around me.

What is your heart's desire?
I hear the music playing; I'm walking down the aisle.
I'm wearing clothing of white flowing softly behind me.
I hold a child in my arms; I see his big brown eyes.

Poetry by April Allen, Senior

Pencil by Kate Smith, Junior

The Best, No More

Poetry by Clayton Whalen, Senior
Tempera by Seth Baker, Sophomore

Look at this young man
He's on top of the world
He's what every young man wants to be
A great student
A great athlete
A great person
At the height of his athletic career
He smiles proudly
It is his greatest physical performance ever
Nothing but happiness ahead

He looks back now and remembers
He remembers the glory
He remembers the happiness
He remembers the sudden end to it all
One fateful day, his body was broken
Never again will he be what he once was
A warrior, a fighter, a winner, no more
All that's left is pain now
His body, his instrument, torments him every day
He lives with it though
And continues to fight
Still the same student
Still the same person
But not the same athlete
The best, no more

The Mitt

Prose by Chelsea Betz, Senior
Tempera by Alyssa Schmidt, Sophomore

I always played some type of baseball: t-ball, softball, just catch; I loved the game. Most of my childhood summers I spent across the street at the "ball park." Each night I dreamt of playing on the major-league field, being the star of the game. I never really had a permanent position until my second year in little league softball.

I must have been ten that summer. For the two weeks before school started up again,

I spent every day with my great-uncle Ed. He was a single man, fixing up an old farmhouse to sell. I volunteered to give him a hand. We spent countless hours working on everything from plumbing and siding to insulation and carpet. Once school started, he told me I was going to have to go back home so that I could "focus" and "get some sleep."

Throughout my stay at his house, I eyed a baseball glove he had there, but I never saw him watching me. The night I was packing up my stuff, he approached me with an old, beat-up catcher's glove. He must have noticed me looking at that mitt and daydreaming. He handed the glove to me as payment in return for all the help I had given him that summer. I was not sure what to say, but I do remember how I felt when he handed it to me. Excitement.

That next summer, I was on a little league softball team just like every other summer. When the coach asked if anyone wanted to play a specific position, I volunteered first: "I'll catch!" I had finally found my position on the field that fit me. I would be the only one with a catcher's glove, for sure. Every practice, every game, and anytime I played catch, I used that glove.

It was the first glove that "fit perfectly." That mitt must have been ten sizes bigger than my ten-year-old hand, but it felt so comfortable and broken in, I could not imagine ever getting a new glove. I wore it out, had to have it restrung, and then wore it out some more. I still have that glove to this day.

My uncle Ed is no longer here, but I still feel joy when I slip that glove on. I don't know if he was a star catcher or anything like that; maybe there was some "special sweat" in that mitt that made me what I am today. Just before they closed the casket at his funeral, I went and spoke to him. I did not mention the glove, but thanked him for finding me a spot on the team. He probably had no idea what I was talking about, but I know he can see it for himself now.

To this day, I am a catcher, and a four year member of the varsity team. I even have a few colleges scouting me. Uncle Ed inspired me, even though he didn't know it. He is the reason I play that game with so much heart and give one hundred and fifty percent every game. That glove will forever be kept in a special place, not only in my heart, but in my closet as well.

THE CARD

Prose by Daniel Meade, Senior

12:37 p.m. My day was just getting started. It was a Saturday. The sun was beating down on the sidewalk outside. I was out wandering around town because of how spectacular the day was. Not a cloud in the sky, birds singing, the middle of the summer. The trees were green, the sky was blue. I passed a pond, and I swear I could see directly to the bottom. I saw all the fish swimming around, as if they were doing a kind of dance. Remembering how dry my mouth was as I looked at the water, I crossed the street to get a slushy from Seven Eleven.

I thought that I would just pop inside to get a Mountain Dew flavored slushy and some Reese's Pieces. I got in line to pay and calculated my fair, which I thought would be approximately $4.23. As I reached into my pocket to grab a five dollar bill, something caught my eye. It was my Permanent Residence Card. I pulled it out, forgetting I was next in line, and had a blast from the past.

The card reminded me of my homeland, Australia. It reminded me of how it seemed like there was never a bad day. It was always sunny and warm. It reminded me of when I used to drive to the beach and watch my dad surf, and what an amazing surfer he was. I had never seen anything like it in my life. The way he glided across the water, then soared into the air, he cheated the laws of gravity. Looking at this card, I remember the scent of the salty air and the sound of the waves crashing into the shore.

The card reminded me of how I would wake up everyday and run around the yard before I was even dressed, playing with Scooby, my giant German shepherd. He would chase us around the yard for hours, and we would never get tired of it. I miss those days, the days when I would get in trouble for the littlest things, but it was ok at the same time. Parents build you up, build you stronger, and get you ready for real life.

My Permanent Residence Card is approximately the size of a regular credit card. On the front, it has my personal information. In the front left-hand corner is a picture of a loveable gentleman. Of course, that picture is of me. The front is a somewhat white, creamy color. When you flip the card over, there is a holographic bar on the back. This bar has more information including my alien number. Above that is a green bar, and in it are white letters that read, Permanent Residence Card.

A Permanent Resident Card refers to the official card issued by the US government to lawful, permanent residents (immigrants) as evidence of their authorization to live and work in the United States. It is officially called Form I-551 or the Green Card. It is commonly called the Green Card not because of its current color, but because of the original color of the card many years ago.

The card is symbolic in many ways. On the back is the green bar. Green means new life or a new beginning. When I moved from Australia to here, I started a new beginning. The card looks a little banged up, which reminds me of the transition of moving to the U.S. There were problems with my dad not wanting to move and us wanting to just go visit our grandparents.

I was startled from this daydream by the cashier and a helpful person in line who elbowed me. Frantically, I slipped my card back into my wallet. I gave the friendly Hindu my money and went about my day as I heard him say, "Have a Good Day!" in his crazy accent. It's funny how a little card in your pocket can bring back so many memories.

32

Different Ways

Prose by Peter Schmalzried, Senior
Charcoal by John Benhart, Senior

In front of me sits a pillow. The pillow is green on top and yellow on the bottom. Age has left its share of dirt and grime. There are four "flippers" attached to the middle. The face gives it an irregular shape, and the eyes, held together only by a few strings, present a comical

appearance. The interior is over-stuffed, making it plump and soft. I own a manatee-shaped pillow. For everyone else except me, there is no point in keeping such a useless item. But the manatee part is not why I still own it.

From 3rd to 5th grade, Kevin Marusek was my best friend. We met at a private elementary school, and stayed friends for quite some time. We were always at each other's houses, doing what crazy kids do. We had a lot in common such as music, games, and other friends. We were never bored, and we always found something to do to entertain ourselves, even if it ended up with something breaking. I was always jealous of his Nintendo and PlayStation, and he was jealous of my abnormally large family. We both had dreams and plans of making it big. We had nothing to worry about, and didn't plan on having any in the future.

Middle school was when we started to have our differences. We started making new friends, but the problem was that Kevin made a couple of bad choices in friends. Also, he had two brothers, Josh and David. Josh had converted from a Catholic to an atheist because of his wife, and David started doing drugs and drinking alcohol. As a little brother, Kevin looked up to Josh and David, but they were setting the wrong example for him. It wasn't long before Kevin followed his role models, ending up like many middle and high school students today. During this time, I moved from Three Rivers, Michigan, to Plymouth, Indiana. From middle school to the last time I saw him, which was a couple of years ago, it all went downhill for him, and he didn't even know it.

I don't exactly remember which birthday it was, but I was given the manatee-shaped pillow from Kevin during our elementary years. At the time, all it meant to me was that Kevin couldn't find anything to give me and chose something at the last minute. It was a funny pillow, and it wasn't surprising to have received it from the class clown. From all the little things he gave me, all that is left is the pillow. The manatee reminds me of two things: a Christian movie called Veggie Tales, where a cucumber named Larry sings a love song to his own pillow, similar to mine; and the other, more important, thing I'm reminded of is what Kevin was when he gave it to me, before his downfall. I am reminded of the time before we had nothing to fear.

When I look at the pillow, I wonder where Kevin is now and if he has changed. I wonder if I could have done something about the changes he gave into, or if I still can do anything today. I know he remembers his past and what he was. The chance of him keeping a present from me is not very likely, but I have the pillow, and I plan on keeping it as long as I remember him.

Examine Me

Poetry by DaLynn Clingenpeel, Junior
Oil by Brooke Poeppel, Senior

Birth Date:
Been rocking your world since July 14,1991,
As an accident, not planned, a mistake,
Premature, but still existing today.

XX or XY:
Fragile and sensitive,
I wear my heart on my sleeve.
Dressed in bright colors,
But arrays of blue and gray
Envelop my mind.

A major turning point in your life:
When I let my heart win over my head,
My world was turned upside down,
Missing my innocence that I feel was taken.

Examine me:
Like a fly on the wall, I am watched:
Dainty and fair with honey blonde hair,
Striking blue eyes that have boys mesmerized.
Growing physically with the emotions
Of a deteriorating soul,
Battered and bruised from the scars of my past.

My playlist:
Like music on your mp3,
A song can tell my life's story,
But one isn't enough.

Dreams:
To get inside your head,
Capture your heart and ride away with it.
The feeling of being complete again,
Longing to reclaim what's mine.
It shall all happen in due time.

208

Poetry by Kayleigh McMichael, Senior
Photo by Kayleigh McMichael, Senior
of a younger Kayleigh and her grandfather John Phillip Engle

Footprints down the stairs,
Lilac stencils dragging behind my small ankles.
A crack through your door; a separation in time.
I followed you through the front porch,
Chasing your bed of white and
Reaching for T.V. Guide memories.
I couldn't kneel in honesty;
Conscience over emotion in a room too green
Or blue.
Folding chairs.
You left everything in the closet, everything
For me, except the written apology.

A clouded rag angel hugged me from within.
The flower-draped bed tried to find me comfort
In waiting.
You wouldn't let me run to you or climb up
Onto your shoulders.
There weren't any mayonnaise sandwiches or
Stick-figure paintings.
You quit taping my "tough love" for 'Crissers'
And helping me with green, clip-on earrings.
I'm sorry for late apologies, now.
I need you with me everyday.
You are, I know you are.

[Beneath the Surface]

Doing The Right Thing

Prose by Marijke Kunnen, Senior

Charcoal by Ethan Pletcher, Sophomore

*I*t is really tough for young people when they are moved with their family to a new town. They have to adjust to the new scenery, remember the new address and phone number, and make new friends. It is even harder for the young person to make friends if there is no one around the same age in the new neighborhood.

When I first moved to Queen Road in Plymouth, I was in a major state of denial. I wanted to go back to my old home in Lafayette where everything was familiar. I could not find any of my stuff because it was all packed in boxes, which were spread out all over the house. Then, if I went outside to play, there was no playground to run to or any face that could be recognized.

I started the new school year as a fifth grader at Grace Baptist Christian School. I was terrified of what the other students would be like. On top of this, my mother drove me to school, so I was very late to class. We took the stairs to the second floor and walked down the hallway to Mr. Jones' room. I had not met him before, but I was hoping he was a nice teacher. My mother literally shoved me through the door after knocking. I stumbled into the room with a thousand pairs of eyes staring at me, and only one pair of eyes staring back, my own. He tried to be polite and introduced me to his fifth and sixth grade class, but he had great difficulty with saying my first name, Marijke. My fellow classmates laughed at his persistence to say it correctly, and my mom tried to right him in a polite manner. But, both of them were unsuccessful. I baby stepped toward my seat that was located at the front of the class. The rest of the day was a bit blurred, but I know I didn't talk much.

As the year went by, I noticed that people were not who they appeared to be. They say that the Christian school has the best mannered students, but I thought differently, at least with this school. The students would not try to get along with me because I had a name no one, not even the teacher, could pronounce. Felling rejected, I often stayed by myself in a corner for recess and would not talk or make eye contact. This was my time to listen.

Halfway through the year, I noticed another student in the sixth grade who continued to stare at me. Not willing to talk with anyone, I wrote him a note. His name was Matthew. He was made fun of everyday for staying in the bathroom too long after lunch and for being overweight. He wrote that he liked me because I never judged him or made fun of him. This was my first true friend since arriving here. We often wrote back and forth, so as not to draw any more attention to ourselves.

Time flew by. I entered sixth grade, and he in seventh. He would often go to the youth group that was with the school because he lived closer than I, and he wanted to feel accepted. I can not remember when, but he wrote to me of the time he was pelted with rubber bands by his youth group. He described to me how they would actually have a lot of fun doing different activities, but never when they brought out rubber bands and paper. Sometimes, the group would go around and do James Bond moves with the rolled up paper being flung off the rubber bands. On a particular Wednesday night, they started the evening off doing this activity. Unfortunately, it was Matthew they were mainly aiming at. Because he was the biggest target, naturally, they shot him. He asked them to stop, but not even the pastor in charge would stop laughing.

I wish I was able to go that night to ask the serious question of why Christians would do such a thing. Yet, I was not allowed to go because I was not a part of their church. Instead, I had to be invited by a person attending youth group, but he would never ask me.

After I read that note, I went to talk to him face-to-face, something we rarely did. He told me that all of it was true. I talked to a couple of other people who attended that Wednesday evening fiasco. They told me the same thing with laughs on their faces.

Sick to my stomach, I went to the pastor who was there that night and asked him why he would not stop such a bad joke. He told me that it was funny and the kid needed to grow up. I looked him straight in the eyes and said, "What would Jesus do? Maybe it

is you who needs to grow up and open your eyes and see the big picture." I left his office feeling disgusted.

We continued the year with

secret notes in each other's locker. Near the last day of school, he came up to me with a box. I opened the decorated box to find a shining jewelry jar with a music box inside. I wound it up for the music to play; he somehow found out that the song playing was, and still is, one of my favorite classical music pieces. I asked him why he would get me such an expensive gift. He responded by saying that the only true expensive gift was the one I had given him which was being different and standing up for what was right.

Me *and* Jimi

Prose by Kate Jenkins, Junior

Tempera by Nekodah Niedbalski, Senior

I have always found Jimi Hendrix's music mind blowing. I'm not sure what it is that got me; the fluttery feeling that never left my stomach when I listened to the outlandish and beautiful guitar solos, or the goose bumps that ran down my arms and legs when I imagined playing them myself. "Little Wing," "Crosstown Traffic," "Foxy Lady," and "Manic Depression" have always been my favorites, but that was before I heard the solo in "May This Be Love."

I had just sat down to do my homework that I had absolutely no motivation to complete. My iPod was humming faintly in the background, willing me to turn up the volume even though I knew I would never be able to focus on the task at hand. I skipped through a few bubbly melodies and stopped on a Jimi Hendrix song I had never heard before. "Why not?" I thought. Reluctantly leaning over my math homework, I let the music fade to the back of my mind. But less than a minute later, I was drawn back in. It was the solo, the burst of emotion, the work of art, the raw beauty that only Jimi could bring to a rock song. My eyes began to water as I let my body and mind be taken by the music. The guitar wavered with a million slides, hammer-ons, pulls-offs, and insane sound effects. Lyrics weren't needed because the guitar was literally speaking to me. I not only heard the words; I felt them vibrate in and around me.

I'll never forget the way I felt when I heard that song. My life hadn't been going well, especially when it came to relationships. But the music seemed to tell me that the release of painful emotions due to broken hearts and promises was necessary, sometimes even beautiful. Now everytime I listen to that solo, I close my eyes and relax. No over thinking, paranoia, or worry about the past, present or future exists in those precious minutes. It's just me, Jimi, and a guitar.

Liberty

Poetry by Kayleigh McMichael, Senior

Photo by Kayleigh McMichael, Senior

I am from a blurry camera lens,
From charcoal-smeared eyes.
I am from sidewalks scripted with verses and
Pull-string nursery rhymes,
From jelly jars of soda held in the
Sandy hands of a salt and pepper memory
And from shoreline messages bathed in clay.

I am from easels and black coffee table eyes,
From autumn floors and doghouse swings
Which broke over tired roots
And a homemade plank of wood.
I am from pant leg confessions and
A classy lady's red wagon
That I pulled myself in until my longing
To meet the grace of her hand grew within me,
From the marble board to e-mails soaking up
The time we've lost.

Autumn

Poetry by Chloe Bugajski, Senior
Pastel by Brooke Poeppel, Senior

I put up my hood
As the cool breeze brushes
Against my cheeks
Silently and swiftly.

The corn is gone, but pumpkins,
Still bright orange,
lay freshly smashed
with their guts sprawled
in the open field.

Brightness beams down
Streaming through the trees
Past the vivid cranberries hanging,
Waiting for frost.

The dog runs
And lies on the grass
Taking in the aroma
Of the earth
And looks back at me
As if I should smell
The sweetness as well.

Not a cloud billowing
As the burning leaves
Present their scent, welcome
To anyone nearby.

The Boathouse

Poetry by Jacob Ladyga, Senior
Watercolor by Alysha Six, Senior

An Oriental Walden
        A gentle winter blanket
    Resting and clinging
        To the barren branches of the cherry tree.
        The solitary life of a man
    Is displayed here in pristine form,
            Simply man and nature in soft repose
Blending as one like intention hoped.
The tranquil pond that rippled in summer
        Now lies dormant and glazed,
    A frozen limbo for the aquatic life
        And forced retirement for the fisherman,
A blessing and divine suggestion
    To stay inside and gaze within
        While the Mother lays her quilt
Lovingly upon the earth.
    A simple shack of timber made
  A modest organic heaven
        Where this soul dwells sweetly,
          The richest man he knows.

Shattered Shadows
beneath the surface

"...Guilt can grow into a monster that sits on your shoulder and whispers into your ear, 'Mirror, mirror on the wall- who's the guiltiest of them all?'"
                                                                    - Jean Marzollo

Photo by Kayleigh McMichael, Senior

Hate, anger and fear lie buried in the unmarked graveyard of the mind. Pry open the lid and hear the screams, feel the pain, and experience the madness of the mind just beneath the surface. Sanity and calm are a thin veneer to hide such dark thoughts and feelings. Dig down and uncover them if you dare and face the **shattered shadows**.

Insanity

Fiction by Kelsey Dreessen, Junior
Photoshop by Nekodah Niedbalski, Senior

Insanity is the girl down the hall who at first glance is beautiful and fun, but when seen through shadows and time is wild-ragged. Her once straight black hair, now knotted and tangled. Her complexion paled and blotchy with self inflicted bruises. But it's her eyes that take the cake, blood shot and dark with pupils too big, the lids blinking at different times. Shadows that frame the face bring out every feature. Lips part into a smile, a crooked smile that sends a chill down your spine. Her laughter starts out slowly, then rises in volume until it's more of a scream. She creeps forward reaching for you. You step back, blink twice, wipe the sweat off your face and turn from the mirror.

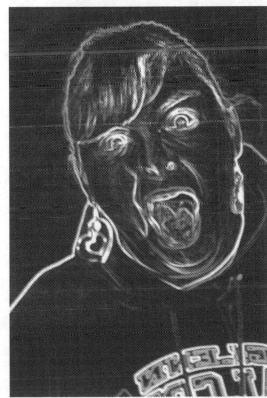

The captain knew something was amiss when he summoned everyone from his crew of one hundred men on the loudspeaker, yet the only retort was a long and eerie silence. He had been trained to handle an impressive amount of disasters, but those recuperative maneuvers all required at least a meager amount of men. The storm had been battering the sides of the liner for nearly an hour now. The liner had been thrown horribly off its original course to the Slovenian town of Kopar. The captain was becoming nervous now and portentously dared to chance a glance out at the deck. Through the minute crack he made from opening the door ever so slightly, he observed an eldritch sight. The deck was bare, with not a soul occupying it. There was no other noise save the cacophony from the constant bellowing of the Adriatic Sea.

The captain was alone.

From across the mist of the sea, he could discern the appearance of the shape of a being whose description cannot be justified by any human language. It was enormous in size, towering nearly ten feet tall. For your sake, my dear reader, I will make a brief and unbefitting description of this hybrid of a nightmare. The thing surpassed the title of unholy. Its form was a tangled mass of what almost looked like the roots of a tree. Beneath this, there seemed to be nothing but a dark shadow. Again I say, this description of the cacodaemonic beast is less than vague. If the beast had not been so hideous, the captain may have had pity on it, for its very presence emanated pain and sorrow. Yet there was something familiar about it to the captain. He remembered long ago in a small, coastal, African village, there was a witch doctor who told a story of a monster matching the description of this beast. Its name was Abaddon, the angel of the bottomless pit and patriarch of a wide variety of horrible reptilian creatures whose claws could tear a man to shreds in a matter of seconds. They had great horns and tough scales. The other sailors listening to the old man's story said they didn't have time for such tomfoolery. The captain, however, enjoyed good stories enough to stay and listen to the entire thing. He was glad he did stay because at least he now knew what he was up against, not that it helped his situation at all. The deck was no longer uninhabited. It was now, rather suddenly, quite the opposite. An extravagant array of foul creatures now began to encompass Abaddon.

Legions of fiendish, reptilian creatures crawled on deck from all sides of the liner. A putrefying smell wafted through the air, making the captain quite nauseated. His consternation was at its highest point. Quickly, he shut and bolted the cabin's metal door as the beasts charged him, advancing at an alarming rate. Surely this was a mere phantasm. He had simply eaten a tainted shrimp. To be sure, he listened intently for any noise other than the pounding of the sea's waves. This was the worst possible thing the captain could have done, for it was then that the creature Abaddon spoke. The words reverberated throughout the tiny cabin with growing intensity. The captain could not discern what the noise meant. It seemed, at first, as mindless babble. Then as he listened, he could make out a phrase the abomination was incessantly repeating, quoted by a ancient man named Hesiod, in every language at once.

"Often an entire city has suffered because of an evil man. The time has come."

Its voice was hollow

MISSING in VENICE

Fiction by Adam Kickbush, Freshman

Colored Pencil by Nicole Noland, Senior

and foreboding. The more the words overlapped each other, the more the captain's sanity began to totter. There was no time to think, only act. In a mad rush of adrenaline, he revved the engines of the liner, and it shot off at a speed that seemed unreal. The captain was cast off his feet, slamming against the bolted door. The liner was

toward what seemed to be a large harbor. As the ship drew nearer, he realized it was no harbor at all, but a city far east of where he was intending to go. It was Venice, Italy. The path of the liner was headed straight into one of its thick canals!

Quickly, the captain commanded the liner to turn

screams died out, the ship charged into the canal, striking a tower and causing it to fall onto the front smokestack. Even with her mighty engines in reverse, the ocean liner was pulled further and further into the canal.

****

Antonio was taking a leisurely stroll down the sidewalk of one of the canals of what he thought was the greatest city in the world. He loved the gondolas and the minute bridges that crossed over the canals. He had lived there for all his life and loved every day of it.

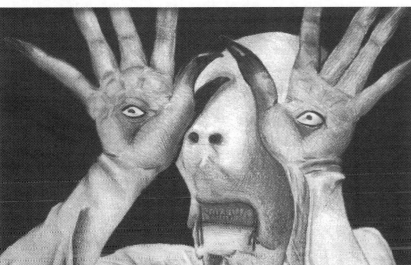

once again spectrally silent. He appeared to be spared for the nonce. How long would it last?

The captain leaned against a nearby wall for support. Then he got an idea. He ran to the control panel and attempted to broadcast a signal to anyone who might be listening, but alas, something seemed to be arresting the signal. The captain looked out the window for a sign that the storm was ceasing. Where there was just minutes ago a raging storm, a thin layer of fog now existed. One thing disturbed him further. The liner was still rocking side to side and increasing in speed

to avoid a head-on crash. It was no use. The captain's hands were a blur as he pushed keys, pulled knobs, and turned levers attempting to make the liner slow down or halt. He put it into full reverse, but that only caused it to move forward at a faster pace. Some other force was moving it forward. As the captain rigorously pondered this impossibility, the bolted door burst open, clanging deafeningly on the floor of the cabin. He whirled around in dismay to meet his demise face to face. The creatures had at last been able to reach him. The palaeogean beings surged through the doorway and attacked. As the captain's

Antonio was an exceptionally smart and athletic young man, but he had virtually no friends. About a year before, he had begun to feel bizarre. He had times when his anger and hatred were so dominant, he would scream and destroy any object in sight. Other times he would get a rather strange feeling that something wasn't right. Once, his consternation had caused him to seize a pole from a gondola worker and beat his aggressor nearly to death. Blacking out from the incident, he had woken up in a mental hospital. Apparently, the animosity he had experienced caused him to go into a seizure. Upon further examination, the doctors found a tumor in his brain. The next day he went into surgery and had it successfully removed. He was now regarded medically as normal and healthy, but there was so much more to the story, and Antonio knew it.

He had researched the cause of seemingly unaccountable anger or violence and found a horrifying discovery. In an antediluvian book he had read about demonic presences. He found that once every one thousand years, a human soul was seized by the devil to be the angel of the bottomless pit until a new host was selected a thousand years later. The host showed signs of extravagant aggression, strength, and intelligence. He checked the dates of these spectral occurrences and found that this very year was the one thousandth anniversary of this phenomenon.

Antonio began to obsess over these discoveries until his friends had all abandoned him. He reasoned with himself that the book had been written as a fictitious story by an ancient scribbler and was to be by no means deliberated. He had denied this realization for nearly a year now. Today was his eighteenth birthday, and it would not be ruined by any bursts of aggression, absurd stories of possessions every millennium, or the fact that the price for pizza at his favorite restaurant had inflated dramatically. Today was going to be a good day.

He was, at this time, traveling nowhere in particular. It had been a long while since he had felt any of those strange, aggressive feelings, and he was beginning to wonder what it would have been like if he really was special. His birthday had been, as it always was, uneventful and lonely. He longed for something to happen. He pondered for a while and came to the conclusion that what he could really use was to see something truly tragic, an occurrence that would make national news like the destruction of something expensive and large. He allowed his mind to wander as he stared intently at the canal. That's when the idea came to him for the hundredth time. Wouldn't it be astonishing if he really was an Abaddon? He told himself, as he always did, that nothing that exciting would ever happen in his life.

He resumed the long walk home. He had nothing to occupy himself with that night, so he told himself he might as well save his money by not taking a boat. The sidewalks were occupied by a few people, mostly young couples who were vacationing. The sight disgusted Antonio. That lovey-dovey stuff was not for him.

Suddenly, there came a low roar from behind him. He had never heard a boat engine that loud and powerful before, but he wasn't really interested in mechanics, so he kept walking. It wasn't until he heard the loud crash and the shrieks of several people before he turned to see an enormous ocean liner crashing through the canal towards him. Bricks and cement were catapulted into the air by the ship's colossal impact with the canal and surrounding buildings, and it killed and incapacitated a few of those couples he had just seen. He sprinted away from the liner faster than he had ever seen himself, or any other human for that fact, sprint. The liner had stopped now and was wedged between two buildings nearly completely demolished by their encounter with the ship.

Antonio stared in total awe. Nothing like this could possibly happen to him. A rush of people filled the sides of the canal. Men and women of all ages came to see what had seemed to be the impossible. Antonio found he was not worried in the slightest for those who fell victim to the crash. He was more concerned with what was now appearing on top of the unearthly ocean liner.

An unheavenly multitude of reptilian creatures appeared and were now lunging off the boat into the screaming crowd of human prey. Antonio remained where he was as, all around him, people were assaulted by the spectral creatures. He had never seen anything so beautiful in all his life. Every aspect about them was pristine and perfect, from their four-inch horns, to their razor sharp claws, to their gleaming scales. He was not afraid of these creatures for reasons unknown to him. It was an extraordinary sight, but was mundane in comparison to what he now set his eyes on.

On the very top of the liner stood the most terrifying, yet strangely satisfying, being he had ever set eyes on. It was shapeless, yet had a definite form. It was nearest to the image of a large, ten foot man, covered in thick vines from head to toe. It wore a ragged black cloak that seemed to emanate a dark aura. It seemed as though it could not be any more impressive until it spoke:

"Often the entire world suffers for the evil of one man. I am he who makes you suffer."

Antonio had never heard such a mighty voice before. It was a deep, hollow, bass voice. The creature spoke in several different languages he could understand. The

Pastel by Alysha Six, Senior

difference with this creature was that when he spoke them, he spoke them all at the same time. Antonio deemed that the sounds he was not familiar with were all the other languages derived from the human race. At that moment, Antonio felt a sudden, spiritual connection with it. He knew without a doubt that this creature was Abaddon. There was, however, only one way to be sure. The book Antonio read stated that the Abaddon released the screams of every soul it claimed in its millennium of rule.

For this scream Antonio

waited patiently, taking notice that all movement around him ceased. He noticed out of his peripheral vision that the humans who had fallen victim to the reptiles had been covered in some sort of cocoon-like substance. He turned his focus once again upon Abaddon. Abaddon knew what Antonio had been waiting for. He opened his mouth, and from it came a sound more terrible than the mind's ken can grasp. It was the single most horrifying sound Antonio had ever heard. It seemed to last an entire lifetime without once calming. The fact that Antonio stayed sane boggled his mind. Abaddon stepped forward off the ocean liner and landed gracefully on the stone sidewalk four paces in front of Antonio.

It was clear to Antonio

what was happening. All that time of telling himself he was never to be anything more than an ordinary human, and here he stood, destined to soon become much more than immortal. Abaddon silently moved toward Antonio and held his right hand against his chest. The moment of truth had come.

Abaddon stared straight into Antonio's eyes. Antonio felt a shock like electricity hit his heart, and he fell to the ground. His vision blurred, and his heart rate began to slow as he felt himself slowly fading away. With his last ounce of strength, he turned to see Abaddon had fallen as well, but was now also clearly dead. Antonio closed his eyes as he felt a terminal chill come over him.

Antonio was dead in a physical, mortal sense; he was sure of that, but something grander had happened to him. He no longer had blood running through his veins. This fluid felt different, more substantial. He felt as though his veins were filled with something supernatural. This was true, for they were filled with ichor, the mineral that is in the immortal blood of the gods. Antonio stood upright and realized he was nearly weightless. He breathed a deep breath of something that wasn't air; it had a tingle to it. The realization hit him like a truckload of boulders. He was breathing sorrow. He was no longer Antonio. He was now what he had hoped, yet feared to become. He was the ultimate hybrid of a nightmare, the Abaddon.

It felt good.

Through These Eyes

Poetry by Kelsey Piotrowicz, Junior
Ink by Brooke Poeppel, Senior

Through these eyes,
I try and close the door
to the hate
that walks,
is read on our faces like a novel
and heard when we talk.
The bombastic talk is echoed in my eyes
as they burn to your core. A novel
idea, to open the heart's door
and let people walk
in. Oh, how I hate
you. And how I hate
to love you. I talk
and walk
alone. My eyes
are closed; your door refuses to open. A novel
of your life sits on a bookshelf. My novel
lies open, waiting to be read. Hate
is a bookmark on the page with the blue door.
You continue to talk
and not read. Look at the page with your eyes!
Listen to what I'm saying. Don't walk
away from what you don't understand. Take a walk
to me. I know it's a novel
concept for you. See me with those emerald eyes.
I hate
crying for you anymore. Mindless talk
only goes so far. The key to my door
is behind your own door.
You'll hate
the quest, but the novel
will be endless. Just walk.
You'll get there fast enough. One day our eyes
could meet. Our eyes could see through every door
where the hate will walk no more and
our novel will talk and tell its own story.

Cold Night Thermos

Poetry by Nathan Gardner, Junior
Photo by Nekodah Niedbalski, Senior

On a cold night, a thermos
in my hands, warmly comforting,
reminds me of us, reminds me of lust.

My tears turn to rust.
My heart starts hurting,
dying slowly of unhappiness.

I think of trust and
you treating me like dirt and
how breaking up with you was a must.

Cold Night Thermos
comforting, somewhat warming,
and yet you killed us.

I gave you my trust
that you were constantly scorning;
it must have been lust.

I should never trust.
I should have heeded the warning.
Cold Night Thermos,
my heart crumbles in rust.

He woke up, pouring sweat and clutching his pillow. Thinking of the nightmare that he often had, he woke with breathless gasps. He had been dreaming of his death again. He sat up and moved to the edge of the bed, grabbing at the pitch black in front of him. He found the lamp, switched it on and walked over to his mirror. He noticed his face was terribly red with sweat beads dripping down his black goatee. The sight reminded him of many previous nights, as it had become his routine. He peered across the room to the clock; its dim red light was a beacon in the semi-lit room. It read 4:20 a.m., the same time as previous nights. He thought of staying awake, but chose against it. He walked back over to the lamp and switched it off. Dragging, he went to the living room to sleep in front of the television. The news from the morning hosts was given in a cheery manner as always. Lame. He plopped down into the recliner and leaned back, listening to the sounds of the city as he closed his dark eyes, once again falling

into a deep slumber. He awoke to the sound of the front door being opened. Startled, he reached for the pistol under the small cherry table next to him. To his relief, it was only his buddy, Lokey.

"You're lucky," James grumbled half-asleep.

" I ' m lucky?" Lokey smart mouthed as always. He slugged the sleeping man in the recliner playfully as he moved into the kitchen. "It's eleven o'clock. Wake up. Another long night I suppose?" his friend said, yelling over the loud music video of Tech N9ne.

"Yeah, had another one of those dreams." He scratched his butt as he stood up, stretching and yawning loudly.

"How did you die this time?" Lokey asked, as he walked back into the room holding a Faygo pop in his hand.

"Man, it was bad. First, I was in this dark room, and I woke up to the sound of a door opening, so I got up." He sat back down and lit a Newport. "I walked out of what seemed like a bedroom into a

room that I think was a dining room." Exhaling the smoke loudly, he continued, "I looked up to see there wasn't a roof, and as I looked back down, I noticed a dark movement from the corner of my eye." Eyeing Lokey's Faygo, he took a sip. "I looked in the direction it came from, and a man leaped out at me, tackling me to the floor. I felt this burning pain in my stomach, and looked down to see a butcher knife buried deep in my abdomen." He lifted up his shirt to show where and pointed to an area just above his belly-button. "Then as I looked back up to see my killer, I saw the face of a clown." He stopped, reflecting on that moment.

Lokey had a mystified look on his face. "So, what happened then?"

"Nothing," and he put his cigarette out in the glass ashtray.

"Oh, by the way," Lokey said, as he handed some envelopes over the table to him, "you got some mail."

As James looked over the envelopes, they read: NOTICE of Late Bill: James Skitz. He tore the envelope open and read the contents outloud:" Notice of unpaid bill on 4-20-2009. You have until 5-21-2009 to pay the fee or your car will be repossessed." Tossing it aside, he picked up the next envelope and tore it open without reading the front. "It's from..." his voice trailed off. Pulling the letter closer, he read it silently, more intently.

"Well, what does it say, homie?" Lokey leaned closer, but James pulled it away.

"Hold up," he stammered. Lokey took no

Fiction by Josh Phillips, Senior

Tempera by Garrett Blad, Sophomore

offense and began watching television. "It says that I've been selected to participate in a sleep study by my psychiatrist," he exclaimed.

"Wow! They may finally be able to understand your problem," Lokey replied encouragingly.

James got up and put on his baggy 2XL T-shirt. He walked to the window and shook his head slowly. "I can't explain it, but ever since I was a kid and my father took me to the circus, that clown has haunted my dreams."

He stood up looking distant, fixated on the memory. It was when he was 13 years old. The circus had come to town, and everyone was going to watch it. His father had gotten tickets by winning a raffle. Being a teenager, he wasn't too excited to go to the "kiddy" event, but he was friendless, so he decided to go. They arrived to the smell of elephant ears and the sound of bouncy carnival tunes. The massive blue and pink tent was the center of the event, so they headed in, father and son. Once they were finally seated, the entertainment began. They had the typical tightropers and the elephants doing tricks. Finally, the ringmaster introduced the clown: "Ladies and gentleman, here to bring you humor and joy, Sparky the clown!" As the spotlight switched, it went to a small car, putting in circles, and a clown hopped out. "Can we please have a volunteer?"

The crowd yelled, each person hoping to be picked.

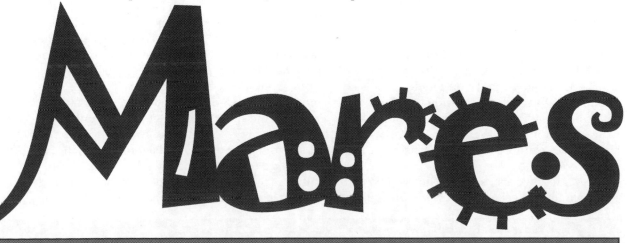

"Me!" James exclaimed, as the spotlight rested on him. He moved to the ring and stood there, slightly embarrassed in front of the large crowd.

"What's your name, son?" the clown whispered.

"James," he replied. The clown explained that he was going to be hungry soon, and James should help him eat his lunch. With that, he smashed a pie in both their faces. The clown turned and laughed psychotically while he pointed his finger inches from James' face. The whole crowd laughed along.

"Hey man! You there?" Lokey shook his shoulder.

"Yeah, just out of it," James remarked, taking a step away from the window. "Well, the examination is tonight, and I've got to work all day." After working eight hours at the steel mill, James retired to the bar to have a drink. He departed the bar an hour later, with a slightly drunken tilt in his step.

Visions of the clown popped into his head, and gave him a shutter up his spine. The cold stab reminded him of his nightmare the previous night. Too many years of his life, the clown had haunted his dreams. It woke him up with the feeling of near death countless times. The elevator dinged, and he stepped out, walking quickly to the main doors. He gave a brief nod to the doorman. The streets of Detroit were crowded, as he pushed past people in his way. He took the bus to the Dreamer's Center, and walked through the sliding glass doors.

"How may I help you today, sir?" the receptionist smiled happily.

"I'm here for the sleep study. My name is James Skitz," he politely returned.

"Okay, one moment Mr. Skitz." With that, she picked up the phone and dialed a number, mumbled something into the phone and returned. "Follow me if you would," she said, walking down the long, brightly lit hall. Behind her, James readily followed, and examined the abstract paintings on the walls while he walked. The pictures featured dream-like objects, strange and surreal.

"Here we are, sir. Dr. Minz will be with you in a minute. Feel free to sit here." She pointed to a chair in a corner of the room.

"Thanks," he said as he examined the room. There was a single cot, with cameras mounted above it and machines on either side of the bed. On the other side of the room, there was a computer and a rolling chair. The smell reminded him of the dentists' office, a fresh, sterile smell. The door squeaked open, and a man in a white and black lab coat entered. His face was etched with age, the lines across his forehead as deep as ravines.

"Hello, how are you this fine night, James?' the doctor said in a rustic voice.

"I'm good, but the nightmares I keep having are still bothering me, and I just want to figure out the cause or causes of them."

"Well, son, that's what we called you in for." His eyes lowered to the clipboard in front of him. "Hmm, it says here you've been experiencing what we call 'night terrors.' It can usually be associated with some type of traumatic experience, such as an accident. Can you remember something that happened shortly before you began having these?" His voice sounded questioning, yet cold.

"Yes, actually, I can," and James related the carnival story to him. As he thought deeply for the cause of the clown nightmares, something else surfaced. It was a very blurred childhood memory he envisioned a little later on the same night as the carnival experience. His father had dressed up as a clown after the circus for a company Halloween party. He remembered the distinct smell of alcohol from the event. After a few hours they finally ventured home. It was nightfall. When they finally arrived home, the house was cold and silent. He was still tired from all of the day's past experiences, so he decided to head off to bed. As he laid there falling asleep, he heard his father ascending the staircase. A moment later, he burst in the door, and James shielded his eyes from the bright light. His father was intoxicated now, and he could smell his father's breath in the air. It was enough to get drunk from. The next thing he knew, he was being slapped upside the head and tossed against the wall. He looked up to see the shadowed silhouette of his father's face, and the clown paint smeared and wicked looking. His father raised his hand in the air, then everything went black. James woke up in front of the doctor. He was sweaty and breathing heavily. He now knew the rest of the story behind his terrifying clown.

"I see, I see, so the traumatic experience you and the clown had may have caused this." The doctor sat back, yawning. "Well, it's about nine o'clock; we should be about ready to begin observation." He set the clipboard down and walked to the bed. "Hop up, then. We'll shut you in and let nature take hold," he said, fixing the bed for James.

James walked over and gingerly sat on the hard, cold cot. He was a bit nervous, but he was determined to find out what was going on. Envisioning the clown as he closed his eyes, he fell into a deep sleep. He dreamt of the night at the carnival, the clown laughing in his face psychotically, but this time it changed. The clown was laughing, but he suddenly stopped, and turned his back. He turned around again, this time with a pistol, and pulled the trigger. A flag with the word " Bang!" came out. He suddenly felt a pain in his neck, and he looked down to see that he was shot, blood pouring down his chest. He could feel the warmth, and as he looked back up, the wicked looking clown locked eyes with him, smiling sickly.

He woke up, sitting straight up and grabbed and felt his chest. He looked to the wall clock: four-twenty A.M. He should have figured. Sliding off the cot, he walked over to the exit. He took a deep breath and knocked on the door. It echoed in the room, and it squeaked open a few moments later. He needed a smoke. Stepping outside in the brisk morning air, he lit his Newport and took a long drag. These dreams had changed him. They made him on edge, almost waiting for death to come knocking. They made him jumpy and quite paranoid of people in general. He stamped out his cigarette and went back inside. There was no sleeping now; they were analyzing his sleep. For the next few hours, he waited impatiently. Finally, at around 7 o'clock, the old man entered.

"We have some news for you, good and bad," he announced. "First, the bad. Upon analyzing your brain activity while dreaming, we have come to the conclusion that you are a borderline schizophrenic." He lowered his eyes and continued," The good news, however, is we can fix your sleeping problem though medication and long term treatment."

James was relieved, yet at the same time shocked. The thought of him being schizophrenic for any amount of time pierced his brain. He wondered how long it had been. What were the signs that had shown them this, and why hadn't he noticed? He tried to recall something, anything. A few times he'd heard ringing; other times, a low roar, like a crowd talking in mysterious whispers. Were those signs enough? Were they the cause of his feeling of being observed and followed? Was the clown just his mind playing a trick? His thoughts spun. Was anything he'd done even real? He got up and took a breath. He walked out the doors and decided that he would not return until he could figure things out on his own.

On his way home, he stopped on the street to get some food. He got a hotdog and took a stroll in the park. He sat down and observed the world around him. He felt as if he didn't exist. No one noticed him, yet there always seemed to be someone over his shoulder, watching and lurking. He looked across the park and saw the peak of a tent, one oddly like the one he'd seen when he was a child. He thought against it at first, but decided to walk over and take a look anyways. The tent was small and fit conveniently in the park; he ventured inside of it and glanced around. He saw a clown and froze in his tracks. It was identical to the clown from his dreams. His adrenaline pumped, and he advanced forward. The clown was creating balloon animals for small children. James waited, then advanced to the front of the line. Finally, he was face to face with the clown.

"Aren't you a little old to be here?" the clown cackled, his voice goofy. James turned to look around and saw a pie on the table.

"No, I just owe you something." He turned and grabbed the pie, and swiftly threw it in the clown's face; he turned and walked out with a new happiness and the kids laughing and pointing at the pie-faced clown.

That night he fell asleep and for the first time in his life, dreamed about eating elephant ears with his new friend, the clown.

Sometimes it's better to ignore the ringing of the alarm clock. However, in life, people tend to stick to normal routines. When a bell rings to signal the end of class, kids leave their current class in school and go straight to another. We're trained to perform, sort of like lab rats. The alarm clock is like that. No matter how hard you want to ignore it, your body still feels the need to get up and get ready for whatever it is you have to do. Avery Wallace was one of these people, and on the day of his twenty-first birthday, he would find out that sometimes it's better to stay asleep.

Twenty years, eleven months, and three hundred and sixty-four days: that was how long Avery Wallace had been walking this Earth. Avery Wallace, the college boy who refused to drink, woke up to the sound of his alarm clock ringing. Sitting up in bed and rubbing his eyes, he slid his legs off of the bed and staggered towards his bathroom. Turning on the light, the hunter green painted walls seemed so dark, making him want to fall back asleep. Staring at himself in the mirror, at the messy brown locks with bags under his eyes, thoughts began to fill his head.

What are you doing right now? Are you out of your mind? If you do this, will it become a habit?

It was eleven thirty at night, and all the lights in Avery's two bedroom apartment were turned off. Sleepwalking back to his room, he reached for a handle to open his sock drawer. Grabbing a pair of black anklets, he sat down on his bed and put them on. On the floor, a pair of pants lay crumpled. Avery reached for the "already used this week" pants and put those on. An Evan Longoria jersey was hanging on his closet handle, smelling of fresh laundry. He threw it over his head and onto his shoulders. Leaving his room, Avery found his worn down, black and red Nikes in the kitchen.

While in the kitchen, he grabbed a snack, a leftover turkey sub from the night before. Avery's hands shook while eating the sandwich, and he was tense. He was so tense that when his cell phone started playing his new T.I. ringtone, he jumped a mile off the floor.

"Hello?" he said, a shaky quiver in his voice.

"Hi, sweetheart. Are you ready?" the girly voice on the other side of the line asked.

The voice was that of Iris Finch, Avery's girlfriend of two years, and a bartender at the local pub O'Houlihans. Iris was on her way to pick Avery up and take him to the bar. Avery had decided to drink after all these years of rejecting it. Since Iris was an employee, there was only one pub on her mind.

Avery stumbled through the front door, still trying to wake up, and was met by a chilly Chicago night. He glanced down the street for Iris's beat up silver Dodge Neon; it was not in sight yet. Avery sat down on the steps and began to bite his top lip. After a few minutes on the steps, the Neon pulled up to the apartment. Avery rose to his feet, walked to the car and opened the door.

Inside, he looked at the

Fiction by Michael Fansler, Senior   *Pencil by Blake Harris, Sophomore*

the
Alarm Clock

pretty face of his blonde beauty Iris. She looked extremely pretty tonight, but then again all girls looked pretty to him when they're going out. Some mascara around the eyes and cherry red lipstick was all that she needed for her face. She wore diamond earrings and an emerald heart shaped necklace. Both of those items were gifts from Avery the previous year. The necklace matched the green North Face jacket that covered up her busty chest. Ripped pairs of jeans were all that she owned; tonight's

were distinct though, with a white paint stain on the left thigh. Her breath smelled of cinnamon from a piece of gum, evidently just put in her mouth.

Avery gave her a little smile, and a reassuring smile was received back. The Neon took off and headed to its destination. He trusted her completely and couldn't think of anyone else to spend his twenty-first birthday with. Avery reached into his coat pocket and fiddled around with the tiny little box. The little box contained a big commitment, one that Avery felt ready for.

"Baby, you seem nervous," Iris asked quietly. "Do you not want to go ?"

"I do, but I just have a lot on my mind,"replied Avery. A lot was an understatement.

As the Neon turned off of Avery's street, he glanced in the rearview mirror and noticed a man walking down the street. In his mind he thought it was weird for someone to be walking that late at night, but didn't mention it to Iris, who didn't seem to notice.

"Is it just you and I tonight," wondering to himself if his friends had a surprise for him, "or will others be coming."

"Just you and me, like always," she answered with a sarcastic feel to her voice.

It was always the two of them, never any double dates. Avery was a well liked guy, and always was the clown of the store. Avery worked at the Subway, just down a few blocks from his apartment. He'd worked there since high school, and the store was one of the reasons for finding the apartment in that area.

The real reason that no friends went out with them was that they thought Iris was controlling and manipulative. She controlled everything that happened in Avery's life. Hell, she might as well have picked out his clothes. She treated him like a slave, but he didn't mind. He was too infatuated with her, and told them all that there was another side to her.

The Neon finally reached the bar fifteen minutes later. By now the clock on the car stereo read midnight. Iris leaned over and gave Avery a kiss, "Happy Birthday."

They got out of the car, and headed towards the bar doors. When they walked in, they saw that the bar was having a frantic night. A bachelorette party was taking up half the bar. The bride to be looked as though she might be sick at her wedding tomorrow. On the other half of the bar, men of all types were huddled around their beer glasses watching the Cubs game on TV.

Iris waved to the bartender, Big Harry, as he was known to the regular customers, and she found two seats on the half with the baseball watchers. Avery sat down next to a man wearing a navy blue dress shirt and tie. He was probably stopping in after a late night at the office. Avery felt out of place. He believed that a few drinks, or maybe even one, would knock him out cold. His fear was that the whole bar would laugh at him. He hated making a scene. Avery had always been one to fly under the radar, not wanting the spotlight. However tonight Iris, the loving girlfriend she was, decided to involve all of the sloshed men in the bar with Avery's celebration.

"What's up, Iris? Haven't seen you in awhile, and is the lucky guy Avon or something?"

"Yes, Harry. This is my boyfriend Avery."

The two men shook hands, Avery noticing Big Harry's bone crushing grip. Big Harry was wearing an ancient, black AC/DC shirt, with muscles bulging out of his sleeves. In fact his muscles were so gigantic, that he seemed to have muscles growing on his muscles. His face was rough, a few scars covering his cheeks. Iris told Avery before that Big Harry also acted as the bouncer, and sometimes got too involved with the rowdy customers. Tonight, he seemed to be in an exceptionally good mood.

"So Avery," the big booming voice of the bartender yelled, "Iris told me that she was bringing you here for your twenty-first." He glanced away from Avery. "What are you going to order him, Iris? A beer? Some vodka?"

"How about a shot of Hot Damn," she answered. "I want to work him into it."

Here we go! This is it. Am I really doing this? Please, God, help me!

Avery downed the first shot. By this time word of Avery's birthday had spread through the bar. Plenty of the men, and then some of the bachelorette party, came and ordered him drinks. As any first time drinker, Avery didn't feel well. By the end of the night, his head was pounding, and all he wanted to do was lie down in his bed.

Finally around three, the only people left in the bar were Iris, Avery, and the big bartender. Avery finally worked up the courage to ask Iris to go. She agreed and slowly led him out of the bar. Walking to the Neon, Avery hurled on the sidewalk. A tomato from the sandwich earlier was evident in the debris. Finally, he opened the door, sat in the seat, and put on his seatbelt. Iris started the car and began their long drive home. As they drove by the big flashing O'Houlihans sign, Avery saw Big Harry locking up.

The car ride home seemed unusually long to Avery. Streets that seemed unfamiliar flashed by the window. He didn't know if he was delusional or if Iris was too drunk to remember where she was going. She had decided to break her designated driver status, downing more shots than Avery.

His familiar apartment

eventually was in sight; the clock on the dash read four fifteen. It took them an hour to get home? Avery was so out of it, he didn't even realize that fact. Iris walked him up to the door, opened it, and led him in. Just as he turned to walk to his room, a hammer was delivered to his head, knocking him out cold.

Avery woke up to the sound of voices talking, and a deep voice was picked out of the crowd saying, "I think he's waking up."

Avery immediately opened his eyes and realized whose voice it was: Big Harry.

Avery looked around the room in bewilderment. Sitting on his couch, Big Harry and Iris could be seen cuddling. The two of them stared at him, big fat smirks on their faces.

Iris spoke up, "Hello, baby. Have a nice nap?"

She began to laugh, and Big Harry stood up. He walked to the lonely man lying helplessly on the floor. Delivering a kick to his stomach, Big Harry knocked Avery's cell phone to the floor by his head.

"Can I do it now, Iris?"

"Sure, sugar. End it now, and then we'll take his money and be off."

A T.I. ringtone began to play, Avery's alarm on his phone going off. That was the daily alarm that got him up at seven. Big Harry reached into his pocket. Pulling out a knife, he bent down low to Avery's ear and said, "I bet you didn't imagine the last thing you'd hear in this life was some stupid ring tone."

Big Harry first slammed the knife in Avery's side, then a couple of stabs to his chest, and one fatal blow to the heart. Avery Wallace was dead, a few hours into his twenty-first birthday.

Before they left, Big Harry grabbed the cell phone lying on the floor. He began hitting buttons, and then laid the phone back on the floor by Avery's head. The message he left said, "A warning to those who find this body. Be careful who you trust, listen to your friends, and when your alarm clock goes off, remember sometimes it's better to fall back asleep."

Charcoal by Catrina Kroeger, Junior

Evil

Poetry by Josh Phillips, Senior
Charcoal by Nekodah Niedbalski, Senior

Evil is the shadow that follows behind you, lurking
In the corner of your eye, made of something sick and sadistic.
It is everywhere and nowhere around you like a silken blanket that warms
You at the thought of it. Heartless and unforgiving, it whispers to you
In a steely tone that is just a tiny voice inside of you
Or loud enough for all to hear, chanting:
"I'm your worst fear.
I'm your favorite.
I'm your acquired taste.
Will you savor it?
If it's blood thirst, will you run from it?
No need 'cause I'm inside of you.
When the sun is spit,
You cannot escape me.
I'm your last resort.
When you have an evil you cannot report,
I'm your royal sunshine, malicious and heartless.
If ever you need an alibi, rely on me.
I am
DARKNESS."

death comes to her

Fiction by Breanna Kretchmer, Junior

Pencil by Kate Smith, Junior

Oil by Nekodah Niedbalski, Senior

"The nights I sleep the best, I dream about being shot," she told me as she sucked down her third bottle of Bud.

I smiled and asked, "What do you mean you sleep best when you dream of being shot? Sounds like a nightmare to me."

She looked up at me from her half empty bottle and said, "Well, Miss Bartender, before I tell you why, you have to tell me your deepest secret." Her gray-blue eyes were hazy in the smoke filled room. I didn't answer. "I guess you don't wanna know," she said, finishing the bottle. Her nails were short, and I could tell she bit them, possibly a nervous habit.

"Umm, my name is Charlie, by the way. Not Miss Bartender lady."

"I'm Jessica. Nice to meet you." She set the empty bottle down on the bar and stuck out her hand for me to shake.

"Nice to meet you, too," I said, shaking her hand. That's when I noticed the scars on her wrists.

"Well, before you tell me your secret, would ya mind gettin' me another Bud ?"

"Yeah, sure." I handed her an open bottle and stood there as she chugged it down.

"Well, ya gonna tell me or what?" she said, picking at the label on the bottle.

"Huh? Oh yeah, my deepest secret. Well, once when I was 12, I stole a pizza from a gas station."

"You've got to be kidding me."

"I know, it was crazy. The bad thing was I felt so bad after I did it, I went back and paid for it."

"You're B.S.ing me, Charlie. I know you are. Now, what's the real secret?"

"That *is* the secret. So explain why you sleep best when you dream of being shot."

"Not until you tell me your *real* secret." She picked up a handful of peanuts and threw a couple in her mouth. "Come on, Charlie. What's the secret, the real secret?" She stared at me again with her hazy eyes. It was like she was reading my mind, like she already knew my secret.

"Ok, fine. I'll tell you, but you have to tell me yours right after I tell you mine." My voice was squeaky.

She grabbed my pinkie and wrapped it around hers. "I pinkie promise."

I couldn't help but feel like I was in elementary school again. I took my index finger and hooked it around hers. "Ok, here it is. My father was a drug addict. I was probably the only one who knew he was an addict. I never said anything to anyone, not even my mother. The night he died, he tried to call me, and when I saw it was him, I … I didn't answer. He died six months ago. I never forgave myself for not answering the phone. I spent two months alone locked in my apartment." I lifted up the back of my shirt and turned around. "I got this tattoo to remind me of him. I loved my father, Jessica. I really did."

"Wow, Charlie. I'm sorry you had to go through that, but you can't blame yourself for his death. It's not your fault."

"I know, Jess, but I can't help but think that if I'd answered the phone, I could have saved him."

"No, Charlie, you couldn't have saved him." She picked up a handful of peanuts and popped a couple in her mouth. "So do you want to know my secret now, or do you just want to be alone?"

I looked up from the bar and saw the look in her eyes. I knew she had to tell someone her secret. It looked as if it would kill her if she didn't. "Yeah, sure. Tell me your secret."

"Ok, hold on to your seat. It's a crazy one." She picked up another handful of peanuts and put her feet up on the stool next to her.

"Like I was saying, the nights I sleep best, I dream about being shot. It's been six years since I last saw him. The medication isn't enough to make me forget what he did to me. You see, Charlie, like your father, mine was also an addict and an alcoholic. He used to beat me. He used to beat me, well... until that night. I had just turned sixteen when my dad came home one night drunk. My mother changed the lock on the door, but he busted through it. I remember the look in his eyes. It was like he didn't even realize that he was choking my mom; it was like he didn't care that I saw him kill my mother. He... he killed her Charlie, right in front of me. Thank god I was strong and fast, because if he would've got a good hold on me, he probably would've killed me, too. He ruined my life, Charlie. He ruined it." She put her wrists in front of my face. "That's why I cut myself. He's getting out of prison in six months. I swear, if I ever see him again, I will kill him. I will."

The look in her eyes showed me that she wasn't lying. "Jess, wow, I thought my secret was bad. Does your dad know where you are now?"

"No, but I hope he tries to find me. That s.o.b. needs to realize what he did to me."

"Jess, what if he does find you? Do you think he'd try to kill you, too?"

"Probably, but don't worry. I've been waiting for him to come find me for six years, and when he does find me, I'll be ready."

"But Jess, how are you so sure that you'll be ready?"

"I've got six years of rage towards him built up inside me. If he finds me, I will kill him."

"Jess, I'm scared for you. I really am! What if you aren't

strong enough?"

She stared at me with a look in her eyes that made me feel like I just asked a stupid question.

"Trust me. I'll be strong enough. All I have to do is fight him off long enough for me to pull the trigger."

"Trigger? What trigger? Oh my gosh,

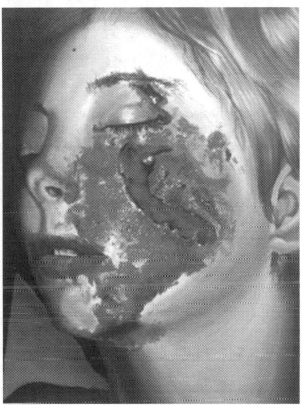

Jess, you have a gun?"

She pulled up her pant leg and showed me the gun strapped around her ankle. "That trigger Charlie. I told you if I ever see him again, I will kill him, and that's a promise." She threw her money down on the bar and got up to leave. "Well, nice talking to you."

"What? Wait, Jessica."

She stopped in the doorway. I ran up to her and reached in my pocket. I pulled out a card and gave it to her. "If you ever need anything, you can call me."

"Thanks, Charlie, but I don't think you'll be able to help me in this one. I have to go now. I'll see you when I see you."

I looked at her, and I knew that I had to let her leave. "All right. I guess I'll see you when I'll see you, too."

Six months passed, and I never heard from Jessica. I assumed that she was fine, that is until that night. I had just got home from work when my cell rang. I didn't recognize the number, but I answered anyway. "Umm, hello?"

"Charlie, it's me, Jessica."

"Who?"

"Jessica. Don't you remember, Charlie? Jessica, from the bar."

"Oh my god, Jessica. I'm sorry. It's been forever. How are you doing?"

"Charlie, I…I did it. I killed him."

"Wait! What? Jess, who…what?"

"My father, Charlie. I killed him."

"Oh Jess! You… you killed him, like he's actually dead?"

"Yes, he's actually dead. I'm standing right over him. Trust me, he's dead. Now, I need your help."

"What, what do you want me to do? I don't even know where you are. Jess, you just need to call the cops."

"What! No, I can't call the cops. I'll go to jail, Charlie. I killed my own father."

"Jess, you need to call the cops."

"Can you just please come over."

"Ok, fine. Where are you?"

"I'm at my apartment in Hot Springs. It's in building Number 4, the door at the top of the stairs. Please hurry."

"Ok, I will." I hung up the phone, grabbed my keys off the hook and ran to my car. I didn't know why I was going over there. I knew that there would be consequences, but I didn't care. I got to Hot Springs and sprinted up to Jess's apartment. I saw the door was open, so I let myself in. I had never seen so much blood before. Jess was huddled in a corner crying, and her father was lying in the middle of the kitchen, surrounded by a pool of blood. I ran over to her; she was holding her wrist.

"Jess, what…what happened?" She held out her wrist for me to see. The blood was running down her arm. I grabbed the phone and started to dial 911. She grabbed my hand.

"Charlie, wait. Don't call. I want to die; I deserve to."

"No, Jess! No you don't! Why would you say that?"

"Because I killed my own father. I killed him!"

"He deserved it! He tried to hurt you. He didn't love you, Jess. He deserved it." Jessica looked at me, and I saw the light start to drain from her eyes ."No, Jess, please! Not now! You don't deserve to die, not yet!"

"I'm sorry. I loved my dad, Charlie. I really did."

"I know, I know you did, but you don't deserve this." I grabbed the phone and dialed 911. I stayed with her until the ambulance came. As soon as they saw her father, they called the police, too. I went out to the ambulance with her on the stretcher next to me. She opened her eyes and grabbed my hand.

"Thank you, Charlie. You saved my life."

"No, Jess, thank you. You saved me from myself. I've spent my whole life blaming myself for my father's death."

"Charlie, you're the best. I would've died if you weren't here for me?"

"Thank God, I was."

Jess spent two weeks in the hospital recovering from that night. As for the police, they saw it as a simple case of self-defense. As soon as she got released, she came to see me at the bar.

"Hey Charlie, how you doing?"

"Hey girl! I'm great! I've been worried about you though. How are you?"

"I'm great, too. The doctor said I need a change of scenery."

"What does that mean?"

"I'm moving, Charlie. I found a place in New York that I really like."

"Wow, Jess, that's great! So when are you leaving?"

"In two days."

"Well, that stinks, but I guess I can still visit you in New York."

"Sure you can."

"Good! Promise you won't blow me off when I do come to visit you?"

"Heck no. Why would I do that to the girl who saved my life?"

"I don't know. I'm gonna miss you though."

"I'm gonna miss you, too."

I walked around the bar and gave her a hug. She didn't know it, but she was my best friend.

That wasn't the last time I saw Jessica. Every year I would fly to New York to see her. So many years have passed since I first met her. I'm 65 years old today, and Jessica is still my best friend, even though she passed a couple of years ago. I still fly out to New York to visit her grave. Every year I leave an empty bottle of Bud with a note inside, telling her my deepest darkest secret.

Feeling Red

Poetry by Hannah Hummel, Senior
Oil by Hannah Hummel, Senior

Red fire leaps up
Illuminates her face
Swirling and whirling
All around are crimson flames
Red fire burns in her eyes
A tiny spark in a sea of green
The Red burns back her vanity
Leaving pale insecurity
Fire burns and blackens her lungs
She can taste the Red fire on her tongue
Ashes bitter and burning
Taking a drag
Lit by some figure in Red

Where Am I, and Why Is It So Hot!

Fiction by Maggie Shoue, Sophomore

Oil by Brooke Poeppel, Senior

It was a cold day in August, and I had been trying to decide what I should wear for my first day of high school. After much questioning, I decided a pair of khakis and a velvet sweater would work, and maybe a messy bun. Then I double checked to make sure all my books and notebooks were in the right order by color and placed in my book bag. I was determined to be organized this year. Once I thought I was ready, I went to bed, so I had plenty of sleep for my big day.

At six o'clock I heard the annoying sound of my alarm clock. Quickly, I sprang out of bed and got ready for school. It felt like an ordinary day until I stepped foot through the double doors of the high school. Down the hall the first thing I noticed was the cutest boy I had ever seen. He was dressed in a slack pair of jeans, a loose T-shirt, and his hair was ruffled. Of course, while I was noticeably staring at him, I managed to trip and scatter all my belongings, completely embarrassing myself. Then the unexpected happened. The same boy I had just been staring at, who caused me to embarrass myself, came and collected my belongings.

"First day?" he asked.

"Um, yeah." I barely spoke, worried I might say something stupid and never forgive myself.

"What's your name? My name is Josh Schafer. I'm a senior," he calmly proclaimed.

"Maggie, but you can call me Mag. I'm a freshman," I said while forgetting to breathe.

"You might want to start breathing again there, Mag," he joked.

"Oh yeah, that's probably a good idea. Um, do you know where this room is?" I asked while pointing to my map.

"Yeah, that's my first hour. I'll walk you there. Let me take your books so you don't trip anymore," he said honorably.

"Why thank you so much, Josh," I said, taking back the air I had been lacking. We walked to first hour talking the whole way, just barely stopping for air. I thought to myself, how can he be talking to me? Josh was the type of person who didn't care about school work, and I was classified as a nerd, and he knew it. For the rest of the week that's all I could think about. Why me? Why did he choose me and not the hot girls in my grade? It didn't matter. There was something about Josh that just awed me. I fell in love with him the minute he picked up my books. I knew I would do anything for him no matter the consequences, but I didn't know it would lead to my death!

For our first date, Josh wanted to take me to a movie. As he pulled up in his outstanding car, my heart skipped a beat. Finally, we arrived in the parking lot, except it wasn't the right parking lot. We were behind the old abandoned Wal-Mart. I didn't know what we were doing there, so I finally spoke up.

"Where are we?"

"Wal-Mart. My friends will be here shortly." He spoke calmly. He spoke as if there was nothing happening. I contemplated what we could possibly be doing here? And then as if it was just routine, he sat calmly as a car filled with deadly smoke pulled up. I had seen the car before, but where? Then I remembered; it was parked in town, and I was with my mom. She had pointed to the car and told me that they were smoking weed and that it was illegal. She said if I ever did that, I would be arrested and kicked out of the house. What would my mother think now! My wonderful boyfriend I would do anything for, was telling me to just try it. It felt as if I were deciding whether or not to shoot myself or live. I loved Josh, and if I didn't smoke with him, I knew he'd dump me. I had to smoke it; I couldn't lose him. He said it was all right and it wouldn't hurt me. I'm sorry mother, but at the time, I couldn't lose Josh. After I had sat there for what felt like hours, thinking about what I was going to do, Josh tapped me on the shoulder.

"Yes, sweetheart?" I nervously asked.

"I promise it won't be bad. I love you Mag, and I wouldn't do anything to hurt you. I promise," Josh said with his wonderfully persuasive voice. So I took a breath of it and right away I could feel the tingles and the burn. I had never felt this way before. It felt as if the only thing in the world right now was Josh and I. I loved it; I wanted to have this feeling forever!

"How do you feel?" Josh said softly.

"Wonderful, darling. I love you so much!" Then in a split second, Josh had my hand, and he took me somewhere I had never been. I felt so ashamed of myself. It was only a month ago I was yelling at my best friend for lying to her mother about skipping Spell Bowl practice. Now here I was, disobeying everyone I knew. I loved it though, because of Josh. I loved feeling close to him. It was as if we were the only two people on the earth.

"Well, it's almost midnight. I better get you home," he said cautiously.

I really should have gone home, but I couldn't; I was so absorbed in our little world. So I contemplated and then answered him with great pride, "No! Forget my parents' rules. I want to have more fun. Show me around town!"

As soon as I said that, his face glowed like the desert sun. He put his car in drive, and we sped off into the darkness. Adrenaline started shooting through me. What was I getting myself into? I didn't care. I was with Josh, and that was all that mattered.

"So where are we going?" I finally asked, hoping it would be somewhere I had never been before. I wanted it to be special, something I would never forget.

"Um, how about we go to the town park?

Maybe we could lie on the ground and look at the stars." Josh spoke with some kind of inflection I had never heard from him before. I couldn't believe he was saying this. This was a different side of Josh. Was he the same person? I was excited to see this side of him.

"Aw Josh, that sounds so romantic. I can't wait till we get there!" I said while holding tightly to his hand.

"Hang tight, we'll be there shortly." As we sped through the streets of downtown, my heart was racing. When we finally arrived, I could see the park, and immediately, I looked out my window. What a wonderful night to look at the stars! As he parked the car, I had to tell myself to remember to breathe. I went to undo my seatbelt, but he told me to wait. He swiftly walked around the car and opened my door. Then with the moves of Superman, he lifted me out of my seat and carried me like a princess from a movie. I felt like I was everything to him.

"Maggie, I have never felt this way before. I love you so much. You are my rock. I wouldn't be here if it wasn't for you. No matter where my reckless soul takes me, you save me! Maggie, don't ever leave me. I would be nothing without you. I love you, sweetheart."

I didn't know if my heart was still beating. I immediately started crying. That was the best thing anyone had ever said to me, and it was coming from the person I loved more than life itself. *Pull it together Maggie,* I thought. I needed to say something in response.

"Josh, that is the sweetest thing anyone

has ever told me. I will never leave you, for you are my everything. I love you so much, darling!"

Then he quickly swept me away to that place I had been earlier. I loved that place, and I never wanted to leave. However, I knew it was time to because at home there would be two people sitting on my front porch waiting for us to pull in the drive and yell at me. As if he were psychic and was thinking exactly what I was, Josh picked me up, and we headed home.

I knew I was in big trouble the minute we pulled in the drive because my living room lights were on, so I started to plan an excuse. I knew what I was going to tell them: absolutely nothing. I didn't care how much trouble they were going to give me; it didn't matter. I was with Josh. I hesitated but slowly opened the front door.

"Where have you been young lady?" my mother howled. My dad just sat there shaking his head. They went on for what seemed like forever, but I just passed the time by thinking about what had happened that night. They finally realized I wasn't paying attention, so they stopped yelling at me and just sent me to my room. The trouble was, I didn't go. I went to the bathroom and climbed out the window. Like a spy from the FBI, I crawled down the street to find Josh waiting for me. I hopped in the car, joyful to see him.

"Well, do you want to have some fun or not?" he said.

"Of course I do! Otherwise I wouldn't have just snuck out to meet you!" I said with irritation. We sped off down Highway 31. I thought I knew where we were headed, but I didn't. As we pulled to a stop, I noticed that the surroundings were familiar. I knew where we were. We were at the county fairgrounds.

"What are you doing here?" I asked, nervous to know an answer.

"A friend of mine owes me some money and won't pay it, so you're going to kill him," he said as calmly as a summer night.

"What! I can't do that! I'm only sixteen! I have to finish school before I go to jail, thank you!" I felt angry to know he thought I would do that, and sad to think that I still loved and cared for him. I had never thought about killing anyone!

"Yes, you can and you will! He owes me money, and he won't pay it back, so you are going to finish this dispute. I love you, Maggie! Now trust me and do what I say!" What the heck had I gotten myself into? I loved Josh, but did I love him enough to kill his best friend?! I stared at

him for what seemed like forever. Then he blinked and gave me the puppy dog eyes. The next thing I knew, I was asking where the gun was. He pointed to the glove box. I reached to open it and noticed my hands were shaking furiously. I opened it, and there the gun sat. Then Josh explained the plan to me. I was to tell his friend Kevin that if he didn't have the money, it was fine and not to worry about it. When I walked up to hug him, I would point the gun to the back of his head and shoot. Simple right? Not quite! My hands shake when I get nervous.

"I love you, Maggie, and no matter what happens, I will always be here for you. I love you!"

"I love you, too, Josh. I have never trusted anyone so much. I will always do anything for you. I want to be with you forever!" Just as I said that, we kissed. It was the best moment of my life. They say there are five different types of kisses. Josh and I had the sixth type, which is all five combined! I opened the car door, walked over to Kevin and went to give him a hug. Then I put the gun to the back of his head. Just before I pulled the trigger, Josh got out of the car. As he did, I pulled the trigger. I did it. I felt horrible. I was a murderer. I immediately started crying, but Josh didn't come comfort me. Why? Why was Josh looking at me like that?!

"Sorry, Maggie, but I just needed a good excuse to go to jail. My mom told me I was worthless, and she wanted me out of the house. So I thought of a plan to kill someone so that I could go to jail for something big. So why not have a girlfriend while I'm at it? Then when I use her to fix my problems, I can just take care of her also. And yes, that girl just happens to be you. Please forgive me because you know I love you. I love you more than life itself. Oh, and Maggie, you should know the number one rule in life: Never trust anyone, not even yourself."

I was trying to understand what Josh had said when suddenly, he pulled a gun out of his pocket, and that was it. The world lost two people that day. Some newspapers titled it "The 21st Century Romeo and Juliet." Twenty-first meaning that Romeo didn't die. Others just said it was just a couple of teenagers who got what they deserved, but my parents didn't deserve it. They said it was the night they truly died inside. Everything they loved was killed that night by everything I loved.

So now all I have to say is, "Where am I, and why is it so hot?"

Sick

Poetry by Kate Smith, *Junior*
Oil by Jana Snyder, *Senior*

It's so hard to slow my affection,
To let down my boundaries of protection,
But you're spreading like a slow infection,
Targeting my heart's complexion.

I still try to brush you off with ease,
But your attentions make me weak in the knees.
Like a body fever climbing a few degrees,
I've fallen under your disease.

I don't want to let you win;
I cannot trust your charming grin.
I don't want to be hurt again,
Can't let you soak into my skin.

I cannot trust myself to speak,
These symptoms lasting months and weeks.
You've broken down my heart's physique.
Love's illness has me sick and weak.

LUCID Night

Fiction by Sarah Stewart, Freshman
Pencil by Ariel Rensberger, Sophomore

"Did you hear?"

I awoke to the sound of Kahlee's distinct voice. The girl was one year older than me, yet her voice was so high, she'd be the best soprano in the world if she just took some lessons.

"Hear what?" I asked.

"That old abandoned house down by Deer Lake is haunted."

Yet another typical haunted house story.

"Where did you hear that?" I asked.

"Shelly Stoner." Kahlee replied. "She's been raving about it all morning."

"Well, there's a reliable source," I said sarcastically.

"Hey, that's not nice. Though, yeah, I guess you're right. Shelly swears by it though. She says she went there last night and saw two people floating right above the lake! Can you believe that?!"

"No," I said. "Frankly, I think she's full of it."

"Well, I was thinking we should go there and see for ourselves, but I have plans tonight. I have to baby-sit. Can we go tomorrow night, possibly?"

"Can we go never?"

"Aw, come on, Ravyn! It would be so cool. Think about it. Our popularity would be boosted so huge if we went there and snapped a few pictures as proof that we went there and—"

"And didn't get our skins scared off?" I finished.

"Well, yeah. Pretty much."

"Who cares how 'popular' we are? Things aren't really like that so much anymore."

"Are you kidding me? It is too like that! All those preppy kids pick on me all the time!"

"Just the boys."

"Ravyn!" Kahlee whined.

"Fine! I'll go with you, but you owe me big time."

Kahlee's whole face brightened enough to blind the whole lunch room. "Oh, thank you, Ravyn!" she exclaimed. "Thank you! Thank you!"

"Yeah, yeah, all right," I said, annoyed at the fact that I had given in so easily. When had Kahlee ever had that affect on me? I must have been really tired. Then I realized that the night Kahlee and I were going to the lake was one night before Halloween.

Inside Art

Photo by Kayleigh McMichael, Senior

Oil by Nicole Noland, Senior

The bell rang, and I leapt from my seat. I had a long afternoon ahead of me.

*   *   *

I came home to the smell of burnt meatloaf. Again.

"Hello! I'm home," I said.

"Hey, honey," I heard my father say.

"You don't have to cook a meal right before I come home, you know. I do eat the school lunch," I said.

"Oh, but you're so thin," said my mother.

It was true. I was thin, especially for sixteen. I was the only sophomore my height who wore a size zero pants.

"I'm going to Kahlee's house," I declared.

"All right," my mother said, "be home by ten."

"Eleven," I pushed.

"Ten-thirty. Take it or leave it," offered my mother.

"Fine," I accepted.

I left with a devilish, triumphant smile. Mom knew that I hated being at home. Crowe and Lulah, my brother and sister, drove me absolutely insane with their never-ending bickering. Mom was being generous. Typical curfew was nine, but my mother knew that I needed to "get away." I felt victorious for some unknown reason.

As soon as I arrived at Kahlee's house, I heard the undeniable sound of chaos. I didn't care though. I wouldn't be there long. I went there often and was welcome any time I wanted to come over. The door was always left unlocked. I turned the knob and cautiously opened the door.

I talked normally, not fazed at all by the toys and cushions being thrown about the room.

"Hey, Karle, you wanna go out tonight?"

His face brightened.

"Not a date," I said quickly.

His face remained happily lit. "Sure!" he said.

Karle jumped at any chance to be with me anywhere. He was Kahlee's younger brother, two grades behind us, but he was a sweetheart, and I knew he had a secret crush on me. We hurried out the door to avoid being hit by flying cushions and other such debris.

"Your mom's not going to get mad, is she?" I asked.

"No," he replied, "she'll be fine."

"If you say so."

We walked outside talking about various things until we came upon Deer Lake.

"This lake has always given me a minor case of the creeps," said Karle.

"That's interesting," I responded, "considering your sister told me today that it was haunted." I pointed to the gloomy looking house on the other side of the lake.

"Yeah, I've heard that before, too," he said.

"I don't believe a word about it," I said. "Just dumb people giving out a scare since it's Halloween."

"You wanna go over there?"

I looked at Karle, and he could tell that I was curious.

"I'm not afraid," he said.

"All right," I said, "but your sister wants me to go there with her tomorrow night."

"Can I come then, too?"

"Sure, I don't care."

"Well, let's go then. Don't worry; I won't mention anything to Kahlee. You know she'll get upset if we went without her."

"I don't care. I'll just end up telling her anyway."

"Okay then."

We walked the whole way around the lake until we came to the old house.

"Should we go in?" Karle asked.

"Isn't that what we're here for?" I responded.

I walked to the door of the house and turned the knob. The door did not open. I tried a couple more times, but the door wouldn't budge.

"Must be locked," I said.

"Why would it be locked? It's abandoned," Karle said.

"I don't know, and I don't really care."

"Aren't you a bucket full of sunshine?"

"No."

"Ugh. Well anyway, since we're here already, we might as well look around. Maybe there's a cellar door that leads inside from the outside.

We looked the whole way around the house. We found nothing.

"It's starting to get dark," I said.

Despite the fact that it felt like a short amount of time, Karle and I had been out for hours.

"But I want to stay and look at the lake," Karle said.

"Okay," I replied.

I didn't bother to argue. Deer Lake was at its best at night. When the moon hit it just right, it was absolutely beautiful. The shimmer of the water could keep you mesmerized for hours.

We went down to the edge of the lake. I knelt so that my bottom touched the back of my feet and my knees came to my chest. Karle picked up a few flat rocks. There were tons of flat rocks surrounding the lake. No one knew or understood why.

Karle started skipping rocks. He threw the first. Two skips. He threw the second. Three skips. Then Karle threw the third stone. It skipped five times and then returned with haste.

Karle and I stood in silence.

He threw the stone again, and again it returned. He threw with all his might, but the third stone came skipping back.

"Umm," Karle began to say, "I think we should go."

"Yeah-huh," I replied in agreement.

As we began walking back around the lake, I saw a glimmer of white in the corner of my eye. I turned around abruptly to see what it was. There was nothing there.

When I got home, I went straight to bed.

* * *

The next day at school, I told Kahlee everything. As Karle predicted, she got upset.

"You went without me?" she asked, sounding betrayed.

"Your brother really wanted to," I said.

"I'm glad we're going tonight then. Oh! Guess what I found out?"

"What?"

"Three years ago, a girl about our age went missing. Guess where she lived? That house by the lake!"

"Where'd you hear that? Shelly again?"

"No. Police articles from old newspapers. The mother of the kids I baby-sit showed them to me."

"So?" I asked.

"So!" Kahlee shouted. "This is a huge scoop, a humongous clue! Gosh, I feel just like Velma!"

"And what's the mystery exactly?"

"Who's haunting the Deer Lake house? Don't you want to know?"

I had to admit that my curiosity had been aroused. After Karle's mysterious skipping rock, I really did want to know what was going on.

"All right. When do you want to go exactly?"

"Nine-thirty should be good."

"Okay then."

* * *

Kahlee, Karle and I met at my house after school. Then we went to the house by Deer Lake. Kahlee had a book bag protruding haphazardly from her back.

"What the heck is in there?" I asked.

"I tried to think of anything and everything we might need. You told me that the door was locked, so I brought a crowbar, a hammer, and bobby pins."

"Bobby pins? Are you kidding me?" I asked.

"Hey, you never know. I also brought a flashlight, rock salt, and snacks."

"Rock salt? What the heck is that for?"

"It hurts ghosts or keeps them away or something. Shelly told me."

"Figures."

"I'm superstitious, so I'm not taking any chances."

"All right, whatever."

Karle, who had been quiet this whole time, pulled a newspaper out of his own bag.

"Apparently," he started, "the girl's name is Lucia Silverbraid. The girl who went missing, I mean."

"Okay," I said, "and that means?"

"Nothing really. It's just a name and a description. We'll know what to look for this way."

"Okay, so what are we looking for?" I asked.

Karle replied, "Says here that she was five foot five, so kinda tall. She had long, bright blonde hair and blue eyes. She was Caucasian, obviously, but her skin was very fair, like a China doll's."

"She sounds beautiful," Kahlee said.

"Yeah, come on. Let's not even try to be subtle. Just use the crowbar," I said.

After pounding the door knob with the crowbar, the lock broke; the door gave way and swung wide open.

The house was no less dreary inside than outside. The walls were bleak, and cobwebs hung from every ceiling corner. The house was bare. The only things inside were dust and the musty, lingering smell of neglect. The house was wearing away rapidly over the years.

"Ech," I heard Kahlee say.

"This place looks like an Addam's Family guest house," said Karle.

"Yeah," I said. "It's okay though. There's nothing to be afraid of or anything. Let's take a look around."

The house was simple: a basement and one floor with a master bedroom, normal bedroom, bathroom, and a kitchen adjoined to a dining area.

The wallpaper crippled around us as we walked from room to room. When we came to the basement, an eerie feeling lingered as we descended the stairs.

"Oh gosh, this is just like a horror movie," said Kahlee.

"Oh, shut up," muttered Karle.

"Be quiet, both of you," I said.

When we reached the bottom of the stairs, the basement door slammed shut. Karle ran to the door and jiggled the knob.

"It won't open," he announced.

"What?" Kahlee asked, sheer terror in her voice.

"Calm down," I said.

Just then, a gust of wind filled the room.

"Oh God!" shouted Kahlee. "We're going to die here, and the police will never find our bodies!"

"Will you listen to yourself?" I asked Kahlee. "Just shut up, will you? You're talking crazy."

A light appeared in front of us, dim at first and then it grew brighter. The figure of a young man appeared in front of us. Then, as quickly as it had come, it dissipated.

The basement door swung open and we all scrambled outside. We ran until our feet couldn't carry us anymore.

"Did you see that?" Karle asked, out of breath.

"Yes!" shouted Kahlee, "You saw it, too, didn't you, Ravyn?"

"Yeah," I said, "that was just freaky."

"Let's go to my house," said Kahlee. "Ravyn, ask your mom if you can spend the night."

When we arrived at Kahlee's house, I immediately called my mother. She gave me the OK to spend the night, and I slumped down into Kahlee's couch.

"Some night," I said.

"Yeah," said Karle. "Did you see the look on that... thing's face?"

"It was a boy," I replied. "He looked so sad."

"True," said Karle. "So, you believe that house is haunted now, don't you?"

"Yes," I said, "I really, really do." I hated to admit it, but I'd be crazy not to believe.

"Why though? Why is he there?" asked Kahlee.

"I don't know," I replied, but I was itching to find out.

*　*　*

School was canceled the next day due to heavy fog. Kahlee, Karle, and I were going to the library and the police station to do some research on the house by the lake.

The police station didn't give us any information. Confidential, blah, blah. I understood. The library, however, held much more information. It also helped that the head librarian was the aunt of a police officer.

"Can you tell us what you know about a missing girl name Lucia Silverbraid?" I asked.

"Oh my," said the librarian, "that girl was one of the biggest sweethearts you'd ever know. Pretty little thing, too. She came here often. Very sophisticated. She was a heavy reader."

"Do you have any idea why she might have gone missing?" Kahlee asked.

"I believe she'd run from her father. Not the nicest man on the planet, needless to say. Gruff man."

"Well, uh... Deb," I said, reading her name tag, "what was wrong with Lucia's father?"

"Prejudiced man, he was," said Deb. "He couldn't stand the thought of Lucia and her beau, Brentan."

"Brentan?" asked Karle.

"Didn't you hear me, boy? Lucia's beau, her boyfriend. He was a colored young man, sweeter than pumpkin pie. Loved Lucia to death, he did. Haven't seen him since Lucia went missing."

"Well, do you know what happened?" Kahlee asked.

"They just went missing exactly three years ago today."

"Halloween," said Karle.

"Yes," said Deb. "Weird, isn't it?"

"Quite," I said.

"What happened to her parents?" Kahlee asked.

"Mother died when Lucia was very young. Car crash. Father moved out of state."

"Suspicious," Kahlee said, almost whispering.

"Were there any clues as to where Lucia and Brentan disappeared to?" I asked.

"Nothing," said Deb. "Case went cold."

"Thanks for the help," said Karle. "Let's go," he said to Kahlee and me.

As we were walking out of the library, Karle turned to Kahlee and me. "I think we should take a closer look at Lucia's house," he said.

"What?" asked a surprised Kahlee.

"I don't think these ghosts want to hurt anyone. They most likely want to be found. They want justice."

"You think they were killed?" asked Kahlee. "How do you know that they didn't just run away together? Oh, that would be so romantic."

"Whatever," said Karle. "Everything to me seems to point to murder. Think about it. Lucia and Brentan just disappear off the face of the earth. No one ever sees or hears from them ever again. If they really did run away, don't you think that they'd go to someone for help? I just know that they were killed."

"But by who?" asked Kahlee.

"Who else?" said Karle. "Her father! Didn't you hear that librarian lady?"

"She never said that Lucia's father killed them," I said. "Even she thinks that they ran away. I could see that happening. If her father disapproved of her boyfriend because he was black, and if Lucia and Brentan really were in love, I can see them running away together."

"How do you explain the ghosts then?" asked Karle.

Strangely enough, the ghosts hadn't crossed my mind once. Now I knew, if there were ghosts of them, Lucia and Brentan had to have been dead. "You're right, Karle. We should go," I said.

"To Lucia's house? You can't be serious!" Kahlee said hysterically.

"I want to know what happened. If Lucia and Brentan were really murdered, maybe we can find something."

"Well... all right," Kahlee said hesitantly. "Tonight."

"Tonight," I said in agreement.

* * *

Kahlee had come prepared with a crowbar for each of us, as if a crowbar could fix everything. I always thought that was duct tape.

When Karle, Kahlee, and I arrived at Lucia's house, we went straight to the basement. Kahlee handed out flashlights, and we began searching for something, anything that would help find Lucia and Brentan.

We searched in silence for the longest time.

"Come on, give me a sign," I said behind clenched teeth.

I felt a light breeze just then, and turned around ever so slowly. There, I saw a vague figure of a young man standing in the middle of the basement, pointing to the floor. Then, the image faded into darkness. I looked at the floor and immediately went for my crowbar.

"Guys! The floorboards!" I shouted.

After prying up many pieces of the floor, we finally made a gruesome discovery. A black, plastic garbage bag that obviously held a body inside lay underneath the floor.

I immediately reached for my cell and dialed 9-1-1.

The police arrived no later than five minutes after I called. The body was identified as Brentan Browers, son of a flower shop owner in a nearby town.

After answering the questions the police asked us, the three of us were escorted home.

As I got out of the police car when we arrived at my house, I spun on my heels and leaned into the passenger side of the police cruiser. "You should keep looking," I said. "I think you'll find Lucia Silverbraid somewhere around there, too."

The officer said he'd look into it.

Three days later, the police found Lucia's body at the bottom of Deer Lake.

~ONE WEEK LATER~

At night, I often go to the lake. I swear I can see two misty figures dancing over the water and watch them rise in the pale moonlight. I was looked at as a hero of sorts now. I didn't feel like a hero one bit though.

Lucia's father was found, arrested, and charged with the murder of Lucia and Brentan. He confessed when he heard that the bodies had been found.

I wasn't happy, but I was satisfied. I knew that Lucia and Brentan were now at peace.

The End

Classified-
Top Secret

THE  FILES
WALTER KOENIG STYLE

Drama by Kayleigh McMichael,
Senior

Pastel by Hannah Hummel, Senior

Loraine: Oh, and then what, Ray? Shoot up houses while on your town-wide squirrel hunt? You've really never been able to claim much intelligence, have you?

Ray: For the last time, devil-woman, I've had it with your tongue and your worn hosiery! (Sticks his tongue out from under a crinkled, dirt-stained nose)

Loraine: Really? A twelve-year-old come back? Grow up, Ray! But I guess that's impossible for a complete imbecile such as yourself... (Ray throws his hands up in disgust as Loraine continues.) I can't believe I fell for someone who thinks Walter Koenig, that Star Trek, Chekhov guy, has been sleeping in the shed out back!

Ray: Real nice, Loraine. Go on and act like you didn't see the clues; the dirty socks, the scattered, hair-like space debris that was nowhere NEAR anything in existence on Earth!

Loraine: (Puts her hands on her head as she looks toward the ceiling) They were YOUR socks, and your space creature product was matted grass clippings that had been stuck to the blades of the lawnmower, genius.

Ray: (Shaking his head and looking a bit defeated) You don't know anything.

Loraine: (Laughs with sarcastic amusement) I'm leaving...

Ray sulks with a scornful expression, which suddenly turns to smugness. Loraine begins packing a few things with rage and heads towards the door, waddling a bit with the heavy items she has selected.

Ray: (Speaking loudly to himself) Grass clippings? HA! Ignorant woman. (Now yelling after her) Yeah, go on and leave! Go run to that fugitive mother of yours! I'm sure she'll have some real good advice for you... (Still hollering long after Loraine has shut the door behind her) ...like stabbing me with a hot dog roaster! (Mutters to himself) Lousy, horrible woman...

Loraine walks quickly through the rundown, suburban streets until she reaches a door of soft, mildewed wood that with its aged appearance seems to have been kicked in several times and maybe even gnawed on a few other times. She slams her left hip against the door in a way that forces it loose with a high-pitched squeak as a portrait of a hippo shudders slightly inside the gaunt building on the wall directly across from the door. Her feet shuffle wearily across the once gray cement floor; her shoelaces are untied and filthy, as if they had never been tied. She kicks scattered, crumpled trash out of her path and stumbles over a hunk of hollow plastic— a Star Trek themed lunch box with Pavel Chekhov plastered on the front, the picture peeling at the corners.

Loraine: (Disgusted) Ugh! Stupid man...(She kicks the lunch box in a way that allows it to crash into and join the other garbage she had dismissed from her view and continues up to a dimly-lit and barely intact staircase, muttering to herself.) What a moron! (A phone rings as Loraine clumsily stumbles up the creaking stairs. She stops and lets her shoulders slump forward. She closes her eyes as she listens to the phone being answered by a low, rough voice. She takes another deep breath, silently through her nose, and continues up the stairs. She calls out hesitantly:) Mom? (The distant low voice pauses momentarily as if listening to something more important than the conversation it was previously involved in, just seconds ago.)

Gladys: (Her voice raspy, trying to whisper) No, no, I have to go. Yeah. I can't. NO. I'll just call you later. YES! 'Kay, bye...

Loraine: Ma? Can I come in?

Gladys: (With an uninviting tone) Yeah, sure...

Loraine: (Pauses just as she comes into view of her mother, then takes another hesitant step) Oh, my...

Gladys· (Sarcastically) Yeah, you look pretty fantastic yourself.

Loraine: Nice to see you, too. Look, I need some place to stay tonight. Ray is on another rant of ignorance. I left.

Gladys: Oh, SURE, come stay when you have a problem. I haven't been so good, you know. I get the shivers still and I—

Loraine: (Cutting her off) Mom, I know. I got your message. I've been...busy.

Gladys: I left that message two weeks ago, Loraine.

Loraine: (Rolls eyes and lets out an irritated exhale) Yeah, yeah. I've been really busy, you know. I'm sorry I wasn't here sooner. What's wrong with your eyes?

Gladys: They hurt, that's all. Everything hurts, Loraine.

Loraine: All right, stop that! Stop this now, Mom! Nothing hurts! You've been at this for too long now.

Gladys: (Another sting of

sarcasm in her voice) I suppose you're right. You would know how I feel, of course.

Loraine: Forget it! I'm not going to listen to this.

Gladys: I hate to do this to you, but you're never here an—

Loraine: (Cutting Gladys off again) This is EXACTLY why I'm never here! You stab a man and then expect sympathy for your problems??

Gladys: He was a bad man...

Loraine: He was a DOCTOR!

Gladys: A bad doctor with a very bad heart! He didn't listen to me for a single moment, just like you.

Loraine: Well then, are you gonna stab me, too?! We have good reason not to listen to you. You crowd your mind with imaginary illnesses!

Gladys: (Bitterly) And you crowd your "heart" with other men's love...

Loraine: (Hostility growing in her voice and expression) How dare you!

Gladys: (With scornful innocence) What? Ray still doesn't know?

Loraine: (Tossing her hands up, the breeze from which brushes her hair back out of her face) And why would I be so stupid? (Stammering a bit) An-uh- This isn't about me, this is about you.

Gladys: (Looking down at her hands) Poor Ray...

Loraine: Enough! You don't know what it's like to be so torn.

Gladys: (Glares at Loraine) Don't I?

Loraine: Not even close.

Gladys: Ray is a decent man with a bewildered heart. He has two left feet and a loud, senseless mouth, but he's never wronged you, Loraine.

Loraine: This is ridiculous. He knows how crazy it makes me when he shoots off his mouth.

Gladys: So you balance that with—

Loraine: Don't say it! I won't hear it!

Gladys: Loraine—

Loraine: (Narrowing her eyebrows) No.

Gladys: He doesn't deserve it.

Loraine: Oh, sure he does. He thinks Walter Koenig is moving into our shed.

Gladys: Oh, dear.

Loraine: Yeah, what an idiot. Then, he had the nerve to mouth off about you.

Gladys: Me?

Loraine: Yeah, he doesn't have much to get back at me with, but he knows how it gets to me when he comments on your... behavior.

Gladys: (Throws her hands up and rolls her eyes) Oh, for Heaven's sake! Loraine and Gladys exclaim at the same time: "Moron!"

Gladys: How about a drink? (She motions toward the kitchen)

Loraine: (Taking off her shoes and walking towards the couch) Sounds good.

Gladys leaves the room. Loraine finds herself alone and a bit drowsy. Gladys' mail is scattered on the squat, makeshift table, just inches from Loraine's knees as she takes her place on the couch. Loraine eyes a shredded envelope on the spotted carpet for a long while, not noticing much of anything else around her. Her eyes drift open and close several times.

Gladys: (Off in the background, talking to someone else) Yeah, I know. She's here. Yeah. All right. Wait.. (A long pause in the conversation) I'm not sure. I'll let you know.

Loraine: Mom? (Gladys doesn't answer. She walks into the room where Loraine has shifted herself to sit up on the couch a little straighter, the way she had been before she dosed off.) Mom, who were you talking to? (Gladys doesn't answer right away)

Gladys: (Breaking her hesitance to answer Loraine) ...a friend. He understands what I'm going through.

Loraine: (Sits up straighter with only the small of her back barely pressed against the back cushion of the couch and slides herself forward, placing her hands on her knees. She speaks softly.) All right, Mom, what is it? What do I need to do to explain this to you a little better? You're not sick. Nothing hurts, except maybe your head from coming up with such nonsense.

Gladys: Would you like something to eat?

Loraine: Ma—uhh...no thanks. I need you to understand what's really going on here.

Gladys: Maybe a nice roast? I could go to the store...oh, I wonder if they have—

Loraine: Mom! What is going on? You're not listening!

Gladys: It's an awful feeling, isn't it? I just want to make you dinner.

Loraine: Wha—

Gladys: (Cuts Loraine off quickly) Ray called. He wants to see you.

Loraine: (Looking shocked, which turns to anger) No. I don't want to see his clueless face or hear his dumb pleading.

Gladys: (With pity in her eyes) Of course not, dear. Maybe you two could say your goodbyes? He deserves that much.

Loraine: What is this, high school? He is an idiot. By the time I finish saying goodbye, he'll start asking why all over again. And I just can't stand when h—

Gladys: (Cutting Loraine off again) He understands, Loraine. He understands everything and he knows what has to be done.

Loraine: (Still infuriated and barely listening to Gladys) I bet he'll—what?

Gladys: I told him everything. (continuing before Loraine can get a word in as her mouth opened after the question mark had appeared on her face) Now, what do you want for dinner? How about—

Loraine: No, Mom, it's fine. Really. I can head over to the Burger Palace in LoQuinta or something. You don't need to—

Gladys: Loraine, it's been too long since I've made you a nice dinner, and I want to make up for that. Tonight. (Holds her hand up before Loraine can cut in) Ray will be here soon and I don't want a fuss out of either of you until it's over.

Loraine: Until dinner is over? What? Do you plan on hosting a boxing match for us?

Gladys: Oh, I doubt it. But just in case, I don't want to ref on an empty stomach. (She gives an empty smile in Loraine's direction, not quite turning to meet her eyes)

Loraine: I don't know why you'd have him here, the dumb brute.

Gladys: (Gives a sly smile) Oh, child.

Loraine: So exactly who have you been speakin— (Loraine is cut off mid-sentence by a steady knock at the partially open, paint-peeled door.)

Ray: Gladys? (Loraine groans and readies herself to walk out of the room, to be anywhere else.)

Ray: (In a sarcastic tone) Oh... Loraine.

Loraine: (Scornfully) Leave, Ray.

Ray: Oh, don't be like that.
Loraine: And how am I supposed to be?
Ray: Nice. (He smirks)
Loraine: I'm trying to dumb this down enough for you: LEAVE.
Ray: I'm not finished.
Loraine: I am.
Ray: (Grimly) I haven't even started.

Loraine falls heavily to the floor, rolling to her side. Gladys walks from behind where Loraine had been located and stands over her. Ray's face seems dully confused as Gladys holds a strangely shaped object in her clenched, right

fist. Loraine's visions blurs for a moment until she can clearly focus on the dark object. Gladys begins quietly arguing with Ray, who has come to stand over Loraine as well. As their quarrel grows slightly louder, Gladys whips the dark skillet in her hand, moving with the rage in her voice. Loraine tries to keep her vision from blurring, widening her eyes whenever the scene above her begins to sway and disappear.
Ray: Maybe this wasn't a good idea…
Gladys: (Shocked and angry) WHAT? 'Wasn't a good idea'? I hope you're kidding, Ray. You are not backing out on me. This was half your idea. Remember the night you found out about James? Or when I came to you

and told you she had confessed about Glen? I wouldn't have given you such information if I had known you were going to flake out like this and leave me with the mess!

Ray stammers his words and tries to make sense of what is really happening— what he is really in the middle of—attempted murder. Gladys has moved to cup his head in her free hand, waiting for Ray's response. He doesn't give one. Gladys still waits. The skillet slips from her hand and she panics to catch it in reaction. As she realizes the pan hasn't hit the floor, she gives her attention to

Loraine who has taken the skillet from Gladys' unsuspecting hand and stands just behind Gladys.
Loraine: (Weary, slightly slumped over still) How's that roast coming along, Ma?
Gladys: (Trying to think of an answer, quickly) Oh, well, why don't you go lie down, and I'll wake you up when it's ready.
Loraine: HA! Do you honestly think you did enough damage that I wouldn't put together what's going on?
Ray: (Trying to save Gladys in her absent response) Loraine, maybe you should go lay down.
Loraine: Ray, I don't want to hear your betraying, whiny voice EVER again.
Ray: Betray? What about those men you crept to in the night?
Loraine: This is your revenge?

Plotting my murder with my mother? You really are a complete imbecile, aren't you? (Loraine turns to Gladys who is still in shock. Ray puts his head in his hands as Gladys opens her mouth to speak, plead more than anything. Loraine raises her free hand.) How about that dinner, Mom?

Gladys' eyebrows pull together in confusion, almost relief as if Loraine had forgiven her. Loraine closes her eyes in disgust. She raises her other hand. Ray has lifted his head to watch Loraine.
Ray: Loraine, don't!

Gladys' calmed face presses against the rough, stained carpet. Vibrant red colors her cheeks as the pain collects there. Gladys feels nothing. Ray falls next to her, as if his caring would bring her back to consciousness. He freezes, staring at Gladys. Loraine lays the skillet next to her. Ray looks up to Loraine with worried eyes. Loraine stares back at him, a glimpse of grief drawing in her eyes. She steps over Gladys, knocking her left thigh into Ray's shoulder as she does so and walks out of the little shack of an apartment with a tense yet mildly serene emotion following her. Ray hears the stairs creak in the distance and begins grieving silently. Loraine lets her feet glide off the last step and onto the once gray cement floor. She pauses to look around, eyes intense. She pulls the door open with a slight jerk of the rotted handle and winds back through the run-down, suburban streets, examining the worn parts of the damp, worn sticker plastered to a hunk of hollow plastic, Walter Koenig's face staring back at her.

Bricks

Poetry by Nick Mann, Senior
Photo by Kayleigh McMichael, Senior

Your bricks are dark against a pale sky;
within your walls so much blood spilled.
I'd hate to have seen you then,
your bricks covered with the ashes of the innocent.

Tracks go through your archway,
carrying the lives of the people.
You see all of this but can do nothing;
you are nothing but bricks.

Blood flows in your foundation,
the blood of the innocent.
It mixes with the earth on the ground.
It mixes with the tears on the ground.

You stand by idle, waiting.
The rain washes off the ashes, but they're still there.
People once again walk your halls,
but no lives lost, no blood spilled.

We learn from you.
You are a concentration camp,
a place of death,
a place of learning.

No Rest

Poetry by Spencer Gravenor, Senior

Eight men, tired and cold,

March in mud, music playing as they go.

Barbed wire holds them like rusty fingers.

Undeserving prisoners watch as their lives shrink away.

Guards aim their weapons, keeping them in tune,

Helmets and swastikas surround them like hot eyes,

Along with the cold ice of stone.

No dignity, no rest, no equality,

Only cold gun barrels and dust.

UNINVITED Guests

Fiction by Mariah Rippy, Freshman
Scratchboard by Dylan Krebs, Senior

The road was endless. Dust flew before the windshield in a thick mass, and even pebbles were thrown against the glass. Words scrambled from a young boy's lips at a ramble, muttering and lipping about how his aunt and uncle just "had to live in the hick-town of Dellsview."

Finally, a gravel road broke the endless straight-away of dirt he was driving on. His hands swiftly spun the wheel of his ruby colored 2008 Sierra 3500HD GMC truck. Yeah. It was a mouthful. All Raiden was worrying about, when it came to his truck at this very moment, was how dirty it looked from all the dust he'd just driven through.

"They just had to move to a place that'd be hard for me to get to. That's all they thought about: ' Let's see how far we can move from Raiden's dorm!'" Raiden mimicked them crudely. Driving down their driveway caused gravel and white dust to emit from the ground beneath his tires.

After a while he reached a few trees lining the mile-long driveway as if in greeting. "Finally, some sort of life," Raiden sighed and leaned back into the driver's seat. He inhaled deeply the strong scent from the cardboard tree dangling from his rear view mirror. It was light purple, scented lavender, with the label of the company at the center in white. Raiden shifted the gear to park and grabbed his black school bag containing three sets of clothes, along with his necessary items (toothbrush, hairbrush, cologne, reading books, etc.). He pulled the keys out of his truck's ignition and hopped out.

The teenager's hazel gaze glanced across the old, red, empty barn, then to the garage with two sets of manual-lifted doors, one open, the other closed, and finally the farmhouse. He walked over to the old metal gate blocking the sidewalk that went up to their house. Everything was old at this place. Lifting the small gate with some effort, Raiden opened it, hearing a protesting creak in the process. He let his bag slide down his arm before making his journey down the sidewalk.

As Raiden made the journey with a somber gait, the front door of the farmhouse opened. Out stepped an older woman dressed in a flowered, blue and pink blouse, and a darker blue, loose skirt. Her skin was aged and weathered, but tanned, and her hair was white, contrasting against her dark skin. An apron with a pocket that went all the way across was tied to her waist. It was black and spotted with flour. There were no catchy phrases, no silly pictures. Just black.

"Raiden! Oh, I'm so excited you're finally here! Here, let me take your bag for you, dear!" The woman eagerly took the offered bag and held the door open for her great nephew.

"Thanks, Aunt Christine...." Only muttered were the words, and ruefully spoken.

"Oh, you kids and your nonchalance for pronunciation. What're we going to do if our century can't speak?" Aunt Christine laughed in reply to her unappealing joke. "Come! I made supper. David won't be in for a little while. He had to take care of the papers to make our new house officially ours! I'm so excited. We live so close to you now, too! It's going to be great, Raiden. You won't have to make your own dinner anymore!" Aunt Christine spoke on, rambling in her soft voice.

Raiden just nodded and muttered in reply, eventually sneaking away with his bag and heading from the kitchen to the upstairs, where the bedrooms were. Raiden figured he'd go down for supper once he got into a comfier set of clothes. When he came down, strands of hair covered his eyes as a result of pulling off and putting on his shirt.

Aunt Christine saw the stray strands and frowned, going to him and fussing over it being in his eyes. "We'll have to cut that rag of yours. I won't let any member of my household have a scrappy head of hair. Here, we'll take care of that now!" Aunt Christine turned around and opened a kitchen drawer containing the scissors she sought. Raiden's eyes widened to the size of saucers.

"What!? Cut my hair!? No, no. No! I'm eighteen. I have a say on what I do with my 'scrappy head of hair.' Now put those back or I'm going straight back to my smelly, hot dorm room," Raiden piped out quickly in his strongest voice.

The woman sighed and nodded, putting the scissors back with a slightly pouting

expression. "Fine, then. Let's eat." Aunt Christine was immediately back to her happy, perky self, setting up three sets of plates and silverware on the table along with clear as crystal glasses.

Raiden sat down in a cushioned wooden chair, noting the smell of roast-beef and mashed potatoes. There was something else, too. Something spicy. He sniffed again narrowing his eyes slightly.

" Did you put spices in something, Aunt Christine?" Raiden's voice was curious, praying it was what he hoped it to be.

Aunt Christine grinned, turning around with a pot of mashed potatoes in hand. There was something sprinkled on top, and Raiden grinned, too.

"I made it just for you, Raiden. Your favorite: spiced mashed potatoes." She set them down on the table, after putting a pot-holder beneath it. As if he were a starved child, Raiden dug into the mashed potatoes with his spoon and piled them upon his plate. He realized then that perhaps it wasn't so bad staying with his relatives.

There were advantages, at least.

That night Raiden lay in his bed and watched the ceiling. At least three blankets, not including his sheets, covered him. Aunt Christine had come in earlier and supplied him with an unnecessary amount of blankets. There were more in the corner.

Sighing with satisfaction, a full stomach, and a small smile, Raiden closed his eyes. After about ten minutes, Raiden opened them again to the sound of a door slamming shut. "Uncle David's home...," Raiden spoke quietly, jumping slightly in reaction to his voice against the still air. It was fairly eerie. "Ah, what the heck. I'll go greet him." Raiden pulled the covers off his body, his flannel pajama bottoms hardly doing anything against the abrupt cold air that forced itself against him. Rushing to his bedroom door and quietly moving down the steps, every floorboard seemed to creak despite his efforts. He winced with each step, not wanting to wake his Aunt Christine.

Between the entrance to the hallway at the end of the stairwell and the stairwell itself was tacked a soft, fleece blanket to block the bedrooms from the general housing area. It compressed the cold air into the upstairs, leaving all the efforts of the heaters lost. "Cold, cold, cold- ah, warmth." Raiden smiled as he passed the curtain, the warm air of the downstairs comforting.

"Uncle David...?" Raiden whispered, peeking into the kitchen before actually stepping in. He smiled when he saw a figure standing before the open fridge, the light outlining a figure in a plaid, lumber-jack-like flannel shirt and dirtied working jeans.

"Hey, Uncle David." Raiden ventured to use his full voice. It was still soft, though no longer a whisper.

The figure turned around, revealing a nicely-built, older man, with a white beard spotting his chin and riding up to his also pearly hair. A sliver of hair accented his upper lip, and bushy eyebrows rose in surprise.

"Ah! Raiden! How nice to see you after so long!" The deep voice rang with joy, and David came over and gave Raiden a hearty hug.

Raiden laughed a little, having forgotten how much alike both his aunt and his uncle were.

"Nice to see you, too, Old Man," Raiden said before getting patted on the back with more force than his uncle meant. They let go of each other, and David crossed his arms, leaning back against the counter.

"So, what time did you arrive, nephew?" The older man tilted his head slightly, intensely listening.

"Around four thirty. Aunt Christine made roast beef and spiced potatoes. There are leftovers, I'm sure, if you're looking for something to eat."

"Naw, kid, it's unhealthy for me to eat so late, anyway," David quietly replied, yawning and pushing away from the counter. "Might as well go to sleep. I suggest you get some rest, too. We'll put you to work tomorrow. Maybe we'll have to bale some hay." David grinned, a sarcastic, half malicious glint in his eye.

Raiden frowned, sighing and nodding slightly before turning and heading back to the staircase curtain.

"Night, Uncle David." Raiden smiled and looked back, getting a nod and a replying smile from his uncle.

"Night, kid."

He smiled and pulled the curtain back, his heart skipping a beat at the small moment of not knowing what he'd find behind it. Raiden flew up the steps two at a time, the cold almost too much for him to bear.

Once he reached the top, he paused, looking to the closed door on his right, and then the one a couple yards in front of him. His own room's door was to the left and wide open, revealing his bed and his pulled back covers. A faint scratching could be heard behind the door to his right, and he frowned, darting into his room and into his bed without a second thought.

The teenager quickly pulled the covers tightly around his chin after curling them underneath his body. "You're acting foolish, Raiden. Like a small kid... ." Raiden thought this urgently to himself, attempting to loosen his grip on the covers when the scratching sounded again.

"Shoot...You forgot to close the door, dummy..." The scratching was louder this time, as if it were behind his walls. He glanced to the door again, still convinced it was coming from the room across the hall. "Just get up and close it. Stop being a chicken," the boy muttered aloud, this time, suddenly sucking in a breath as he heard a door slam. He was sure his uncle was in bed...wasn't he? Raiden scowled and shoved the covers off again, despite his shivering body. "Shut up and stop being a fool. You're going back downstairs to see who went where."

Once Raiden got to his door, he froze, nothing making a sound. The heaters that were going downstairs, their old mechanical bodies loud and obtrusive, weren't even making the familiar hum they usually did. The scratching was gone, but the door before him was cracked open slightly.

Raiden ran down the stairs, passing through the blanket hanging as a curtain and letting it mess his hair. He peeked into his aunt and uncle's bedroom; its door open, as it usually was. He turned around, rather than passing through their bedroom, and went into the kitchen, glancing around and looking to the front door. Next to the front door was a pantry area consisting of shelves, trash cans, and a door to the cellar.

Unwilling to venture into the small square of space quite yet, Raiden passed through the kitchen and into the dining area. The long dining table was clustered with bills and letters, along with old anniversary and birthday cards. "Sheesh. For only living here for a month, the two really have made themselves at home," Raiden quietly said to himself, before looking up through the wide entryway leading to the den.

Hidden in the darkness were a couch, a short coffee table, a television set, and a giant grandfather clock in the corner behind the couch. Glancing up, he spotted his reflection in the television screen, causing him to jump about a foot in the air before ducking behind one of the antique chairs pushed beneath the dining table.

Waiting for some sort of beast, Raiden squeezed his eyes shut. After a minute or so, Raiden opened his eyes, nothing surrounding him but the air itself, and stood up. Warily, he ventured into the den and up to the glistening TV screen, putting his hand up against it with a smirk and a hesitant laugh. He turned around and glanced at the grandfather clock, its abrupt ring sending him flying to the ground beneath the coffee table. "Dong, Dong, Dong, Dong, Dong, Dong, Dong, Dong, Dong, Dong, Dong, Dong." Right when he thought it would never end, it did, at the number twelve.

"Dang, Twelve already...I'm going to be exhausted tomorrow. Maybe they'll realize I'm a teenager and let me sleep in." This thought rushed through his mind hastily, and he huffed out a laugh. Getting back to his feet in utter embarrassment, Raiden was grateful nobody had been there with him.

As quietly as possible, he suffered his way through the dark dining room, his nerves on edge from the pitch-blackness. He re-entered the kitchen, just about to get to the staircase, when he remembered the pantry and his former destination.

"Someone slammed that door...," Raiden quietly mumbled, turning around so he could see the front door. "I'm sure it's just..." Cutting off in mid-sentence, Raiden glanced to his aunt and uncle's room. He could make out the loud, guttural snore of his uncle and the softer breathing of his aunt.

Heading to the front door, he carefully opened it, and was immediately greeted by the freezing night air. Everything seemed to be in place. The cellar door, too, was closed. Raiden was beginning to think he imagined it all.

Turning around, willing to forget about it and the cellar door, he froze, yet again, to the noise of scratching. Squeezing his eyes shut, and pulling his arms tightly to his chest, he shrank in his socks. "Please, not the cellar. Please, oh please." As he listened further, he noticed the scratching was coming from behind him, and he turned around just slightly, popped his eyes open, and faced the cellar door.

"Just my luck," he firmly said through clenched teeth. He could feel his legs go flimsy and his heart begin to flutter. "They're just rats, I'm sure. I'll go downstairs and find traps and chewed boxes." Raiden continued to rant under his breath, reassuring himself that it wasn't like all the horror books he'd read and all the movies he'd seen.

He opened the cellar door. It was a plain, withered wooden door. Its handle, though, seemed to be colder than the outside air, numbing his hand, even from the short amount of time it rested against it. Before him were the stone stairs, heading down to the darkest room he'd ever seen. Conveniently set beside the stairs was a railing leading down into the depths of darkness. Raiden looked around for a light switch. Unfortunately for him, the light was merely a light bulb, turned on by a cord dangling from a fixture in the middle of the cellar.

Taking one step at a time, as wary as ever, Raiden began his way down into the cellar, noting as he got farther down the steps, that it wasn't as dark as he thought. There was a small basement window, about the size of a bread basket, letting in the light of the moon. It was full and shining brightly. As he looked around, using the moonlight as his source to see, he noticed that a large tarp was rolled up in the corner, resting beside an abnormally small door. Raiden's mind didn't comprehend the abnormality before passing onto other objects. There was an old snow ski hanging from a nail near the ceiling, and as he looked further to the right, he saw a shelf containing many spices and a few bottles of vinegar. There was also a box of junk sitting a few feet away from the wall. The boy leaned over the railing and spotted a stack of newspapers, probably about as old as the house, and beside them an old-fashioned radio.

"I wonder if this stuff is theirs or if it belonged to the person who lived here before," Raiden quietly pondered, sighing with slight relief and beginning to turn around. Before he could finish his sigh of relief, it caught in his throat, and all his nerves suddenly jumped off the edge they'd been standing on. From the corner of his eye, he saw the one thing he was subconsciously avoiding. His heart was pounding; he was sure he had seen the door knob turn. Without another thought, he turned and skipped as many stone steps as he could manage, racing for the door at the top of the stairs. It slammed closed, just like the slams he'd heard before, though this time it was loud and made his ears ring. Raiden jumped back with a stifled gasp, missed the step he'd been aiming for, and fell back down, slamming against the painful steps until he reached the hard floor. He was sure he'd broken nearly half his body. He couldn't feel a thing and was unable to move. His eyes darted to the ceiling, the beams taunting him with their size and vast length.

Quietly, like a mouse, a creak interrupted his wishful thinking. His eyes darted to the area behind his head and saw a shadow, a mountainous shadow.

Mustiness was in the air, the scent like wet clothes and a fall day mixed into one.

For the last time, Raiden squeezed his eyes shut.

Outside *Inside*

Poetry by Ethan Wolfe, Senior
Oil by Chris Wenger, Senior

On the Outside
I pretend that nothing affects me,
nothing bothers me,
and that I'm all right
when someone
makes fun of me.
It used to hurt.
I would get sad
and depressed.
Now
I'm used to it.
I hide it
even from myself.

On the Inside
I am crushed,
then sad,
then angry.
I think,
"I'm a good person;
I don't deserve this."
There is a bubble inside of me
each time I'm made fun of.
It gets bigger
and bigger
and bigger
till I think it will burst.
I think someday it will.

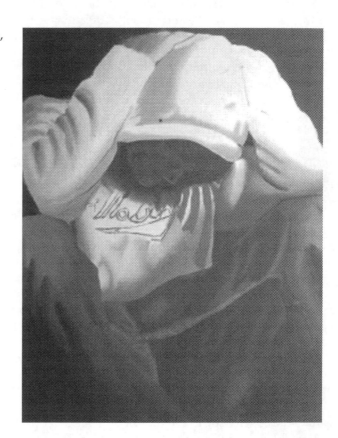

The *Web* of *My Life*

Poetry by Nathan Gardner, Junior
Photoshop by Chris Wenger, Senior

Name:
My name is the word on the tongues of the dead
My name is the quiet before the storm
My name is constant desolation
You hate my name like poison
But need it like drugs

Address:
Here but also there
Live yet also dead
Under the overpass
Over your roof
In all the books in the library
Ultimately alone

Career Plan:
In the clockwork
Over her
Helping others
To be miserable like me
Marriage counselor
Divorced

Religion:
I hear a voice in my head
It tells me to do things
I listen to it sometimes
It only happened once
Never again
When I die
I rot in Technicolor
Beautiful
Bastardized
I drink my religion
I bleed for dreams

Family Life:
I have a family
They live in bloody matrimony
In the sky
Under the tree
We all die

Graced by Death

Poetry by Heather Helminger, Senior
Tempera by Ethan Pletcher, Sophomore

The wind brings the stifled
Air of the decomposed,
And breathing is subduing yourself
To its fate.
Manifested upon the bodies,
A look so lucid that
It makes the crows cry.
I walk through the valley
Of death, my home,
Red draped over doorways
Of the condemned.
Never say goodbye.
I pray that these poor souls
Find peace through this plague,
Wiping out every victim that dares
To cross its path.
I can't believe the sound of the screams
That fall on me from the windows.
Lucky are the ones who stay alive
And overcome insanity.
Oh God,
Why must you ignore our calls?
Your very followers brought into
The pits of Hell,
Pleading for me to help them. Me...
I am blessed to be alive.
Nobody has the skill to help them.
They are doomed,
And I am tortured
To watch.
The sky comes closer as
The earth sinks into the ground.
Time is our anonymous villain,
Creeping in unexpectedly.
Hope falls into the pits
Dug for the dead, and
Hopelessness is the future
That we find.
I only hope that the
Cure will be found to
Keep the clocks ticking.

Winter Sorrows

Poetry by Bryan Sporner, Sophomore
Photo by Hannah Hummel, Senior

Looking down at the winter snow
as I sit here thinking of you,
I suddenly feel a crimson flow,
and yet I have no clue.

As I sit here thinking of you
I wonder what happened, how could it be,
yet still I have no clue.
Could my love have come with such a fee?

Still I wonder how could it be
as I look around and see some blood.
Is this how love can set me free?
Now the snow is mixed like water to mud.

I get dizzy looking at the puddle of blood
as I feel the crimson river flow.
More snow is now mixed like water to mud;
slowly I sink into winter's slumber below.

Hearts and Minds
beneath the surface

"The face is the mirror of the mind, and eyes without
speaking confess the secrets of the heart."
- Saint Jerome

Photo by Kayleigh McMichael, Senior

Love stays warm, sheltered in the secret chambers of the heart, mind, and soul. Knock softly on Love's door and be welcomed into the passion and friendship beneath the surface. Love, be it romantic, platonic, or spiritual whispers our private thoughts and feelings to those who yearn and listen. Delve down and embrace the secrets of **hearts and minds.**

I'll Be Here with You

Poetry by Kayleigh McMichael, Senior

Photo by Kayleigh McMichael, Senior

Kelly blue eyes wake me with "I love you"
      as you drift quietly from under the
      blankets and break the shadows
      covering my face.
An illusion of time, or last fall, fills me. You
      step backwards into my fight against
      sleep. August 16th as a field of stones.
      Water, like floors accidentally
      patterned with the camera you held
      for six familiar years. There, a
Yellow Victorian house yawning quiet resentment,
Leaving to the future layered warmth
      absorbed in a scarf too long and a
      jacket pulling black and white from
      its every surrounding. The light
      reawakens me to space; a room where
Empty frames spill over me as I etch
      prayer into bamboo ceilings. Eggshell
      pride ripples beneath the glow of
      waking exhales. My hand moves across
      my face in search of color.
Indigo haze hanging over green eyes, naturally
      dark, like yours, with a nose to match.
Guarded by the city lights, I dream in
      color. I carry with me the world, for
      what it is, reciting
Hallelujah pick-me-ups that hold me
      within you. The dip in your chest
      fits me as we sing out of tune,
      I'll be here with you.

What GRANDPA Taught Me About LOVE

Prose by Jessica Downey, Senior

I first learned about what love is from my grandpa. I have always been especially close to my grandpa Downey; he had a special liking for me that he never had with any of the other kids in the family. My grandpa and I always share stories, and one particular story that always sticks in my mind is the story of how he and Grandma got together.

It all started one summer after my grandpa hitchhiked all the way to Indiana from Iowa. He didn't like it in Iowa anymore. He knew he had family up here, so he decided to run away from home. It was the summer before his senior year in high school. When he got here, he called his family to tell them where he was and that he was ok. My great-grandparents were furious, of course, but understanding and followed his lead. Shortly after moving here, he laid eyes on my grandma. My grandmother's name at the time was Edna Lucille Walters, and he thought it was the most beautiful name in the world. My grandma worked at the ice cream parlor. It was a little stand set up outside the movie theater near where Subway is now in Walkerton. My grandpa would always go to get ice cream, maybe four or five times a night, and my grandma found it quite ridiculous. Then one day he worked up the courage to ask her out.

He went up to her and said, "Hi Edna. I'm Neil, and you're going on a date with me." Grandma was very shy, and knew that her best friend had a crush on my grandpa, so she refused. Grandpa, however, was adamant. Grandma's friend told her to go out with him because she would end up marrying him.

That night, Grandpa went to the ice cream parlor and asked her out again. She, of course, said no again, but he was a persistent man and always, I mean always, gets what he wants. Around this time period, there was a popular song out called "Lucille." This just so happened to be Grandma's middle name. So what did my crazy grandpa do? He started belting this song out in the parking lot in front of everyone. Grandma was quickly embarrassed, and said, "I will go out with you if you shut the heck up!" So he did, and they went out.

Shortly after being together, they decided they to get married and did in December of 1947. Grandma "looked like a diamond in the rough," as Grandpa always described it. Grandpa then went off to the Navy, and Grandma had their first child.

My great-grandmother lived with them until she passed, and Grandma said she put a great damper on their relationship at times, but nothing could ever change the love she has for my grandpa. My grandparents are now in their eighties. Grandpa suffers from Parkinson's disease, and Grandma from Alzheimer's, yet their love is still so proud and true. They still give each other kisses goodnight, and tell each other they love one another. This amazing story of love and commitment has influenced me greatly.

Knowing that this is possible, I will not be happy until I find the man my grandpa is. My grandpa is my best friend and will always get the credit for showing me what true love is. He tells me that times aren't always going to be easy, but as soon as you have the one you love by your side, everything will work out.

Grandpa Tom

Poetry by Chloe Bugajski, Senior
Photo of Chloe and Grandfather Tom

I was barely three years old
And you, in your fifties.
Christmas at Aunt Ruth's
Was tradition like every other year.
My hands are gripped on your throat,
Smile crossing my face,
But I'm not hurting you
Nor am I intending to.
Just wanted to touch you, feel your love,
Feel Grandpa.
You're holding me in your arms,
Glasses covering your eyes,
And modeling one of your many classic
sweaters.

That was four years before you passed.
Even though now I can't grip your throat,
I can still feel you
Smell you
Hear you
And see you in my dreams.
I've changed a lot, but I'm still
"Grandpa's little girl."

Not a day goes by that I don't
Look at your picture
And think of you.
You may not be here for me physically,
But I'm living for you,
And you're living on through me.

I awoke, hoping it had all been a dream. I wanted the past weeks to have been only a nightmare- Emma's medication failing, the violent outbursts and hallucinations coming back, her schizophrenia taking her away. The last episode she had before she left kept replaying in my head like a broken record. Her chaotic screaming reverberated in my mind. It had been the third time treatments hadn't worked. I'd lost faith. I'd lost my wife.

The sun poured through my windows as I looked to my clock and realized it was 3:30 in the afternoon. Another day had passed. As my eyes adjusted to the brilliant sunlight, I looked around my childhood room. Although I had an apartment of my own, my concerned family felt it necessary that I stay with them at our rather large lake house until I became emotionally stable again. With no strength left to argue, I was forced to agree. My room had not changed since I left it only a few years earlier. My soccer trophies sat gleaming on their shelf, the pictures of family and friends smiled back at me in their frames, and the collage Emma had made me for our one year anniversary in high school hung on the wall near the window. My chest began to ache at the very sight of it. I barely left the room for two weeks, contemplating the decision I had to make between the lost girl I loved and the life I wanted back. It was time.

I got out of bed and walked to the mirror next to my door. My reflection stared back at me with miserable weakness. I rubbed my tired, red eyes and tousled my shaggy hair realizing how badly it needed cut. Rubbing my jaw, I also realized I needed to shave desperately. On my way to the bathroom, my sister's over-filled school bag made me fall flat on my face.

Violet was the most intellectual person I knew, next to our parents, and she was only sixteen at the time. She not only acted as though she was an adult, she looked like one. It scared the hell out my father and I. Her soft face was contradicted by the dark, edgy, brunette bob that framed it. With a simple style, she was the model of sophistication. Whenever Vi wasn't wearing her glasses, you could see those bright green eyes we had both inherited from our mother. She impressed me more and more everyday with her growing grace and maturity. Earlier that week, Violet had stopped me in the kitchen amidst one of my ventures from my room for food. She approached me nonchalantly and simply said, "Don't feel guilty. She isn't the same Emma we all knew and loved anymore. You have a right to feel the way you do. I just wanted you to know that." And with that, she walked back to the table and resumed her homework, not knowing how much I'd needed someone's approval at the time.

After I'd finally made it to the shower and taken care of my personal hygiene, I made my way downstairs to the den. My mother sat typing away at her computer working on her latest novel. Her writing had once been described as an intriguing blend of Jane Austen and J.D. Salinger. As soon as I entered

Fiction by Kelsey Piotrowicz, Junior

Pastel by Nicole Noland, Senior

the room, her head perked up above the computer with a look of great surprise, and she hurriedly began to tidy the wild array of papers dispersed on her desk. That day, she had been dressed in a flowing olive green tunic, with a number of multicolored bracelets on both wrists. Her graying blonde hair was pulled up into a messy bun of uncontrollable curls. For a woman of fifty, she was quite attractive. She took her thick framed glasses down from where they were perched on her nose and gave me an empathetic smile.

"How are ya sweetie? I'm glad to see you're up and dressed. You've even shaved!" she said, with an unnecessary amount of vigor.

"I'm going, "I replied. Her smile then turned into a look of earnest compassion.

"Would you like me to go with you?" she asked.

"No, no. The paperwork went through the court and was just approved. I'm just going to get her doctor's signature, and it'll be done. Linda and Paul know. They came over yesterday while you were all at church. They said they were hoping I would make this decision with myself in mind. They said it's what their daughter would've wanted." I paused not sure I could go on. "I just can't do it, Mom. I can't see her like this, and I can't take care of her anymore. She's not the girl I loved. When she was first diagnosed two years ago, I

thought maybe there was hope she'd be able to maintain it. I guess ever since her first round of medications stopped working though, I knew it would end up like this. I miss her, but I can't see this side of her everyday anymore." Almost unable to speak, the tears began to fall.

"Eric, you're twenty-four years old. You have your whole life ahead of you still. You know if the real Emma could see the situation, she'd

tell you to end it and get the divorce because she loved you. She never wanted anything but the best for her husband. Emma wouldn't want this for you. She'd want you to move on with your life. You are doing the right thing,. OK, sweetie. You are." She too began to cry, and she quickly got up and threw her arms around me tenderly. I felt as though I was a child again. It was as if I'd fallen off my bike and my

mom had to come rushing to console me. After a couple of seconds, I pulled away and told my mother goodbye. Grabbing my keys, I walked to my green sedan parked in the four car garage.

I met my father getting out of his car. It was a little after four, so he must have gotten home early from the office for some reason. Dressed in his charcoal gray suit, he was the epitome of refinement.

Before I could even get a word out, he set his briefcase down and gave me a powerful hug. He knew where I was going, but he said nothing. It wasn't that he didn't care or was unsure of what to say; instead, he was intuitive enough to comprehend I needed no more than the knowledge of his support. I've learned the strong and silent are normally also the wisest. After a couple of pats on my back, he let go, picked up his briefcase and walked to the house. That was the type of man I wanted to be.

The drive to the hospital was torturous. The silence, unbearable. I pressed the power button on the radio. Realizing my mother had last had the car, I understood why the oldies station came blaring through the speakers. Paul McCartney's voice sang a familiar song: "And anytime you feel the pain, hey Jude, refrain. Don't carry the world upon your shoulders. For well you know that it's a fool who plays it cool by making his world a little colder...." My mother sang that song every holiday as she cooked. The words never meant more than they did in that moment. That recognizable ache came in my chest yet again. I rolled down the window to breathe in some of the early autumn air and kept driving.

I soon arrived and walked through the automatic doors as they opened. St. Francis Hospital had remained the same since Emma's first trip there. This being her third time admitted, I could have walked the corridors blindfolded. Rita, the kind receptionist I'd come to know, greeted and directed me to Dr. Triste's personal office. I walked quickly, just wanting to end all of it. The meeting went as well as could be expected.

"The memory of her illness remains seated there, a false interpretation of who she was."

Dr. Triste was very considerate and signed the papers with silent understanding.

I saw Emma that day. She was happy to see me. We talked for awhile about simple things- the weather, TV shows, the people she'd met during her stay. I was instructed not to talk to her about the matter at hand for fear it would induce too much stress on her neurological system. Someone would explain the divorce to her at a later date. Unfortunately, that day wasn't a good day, even despite not telling her about the situation. She started having another fit, and that was my cue to leave.

I was walking back to my car when I suddenly felt an overwhelming wave of fatigue. A bench loomed in the distance. I decided to sit. My mind wandered through the life Emma and I had shared together- college, graduations, our wedding, holidays, arguments, laughing fits, sex, and love. It had all been so extraordinary. I would always love her. She was part of me.

As I walked away, I left something on that bench. The memory of her illness remains seated there- a false interpretation of who she was. Emma wasn't the dim point in my life. She was the light that led me to who I've become.

"Jacqueline Jordan! Get out'ta bed now!" That's pretty much what I have heard every morning for the past twelve years. I'm not a morning person. My mother was always screaming at me to get moving. I hated school and had absolutely no motivation. If it hadn't been for my mom, I probably would have dropped out my sophomore year.

My mom has always been a pusher, and she has always been a doer. She owns her own business, helps my dad manage his own business, raises a family, and has taken care of both my ill grandmothers. She doesn't let difficult times get her down; when things get rough, that's when she buckles down harder. My mom always told me to set a goal for myself and never lose sight of it; if I'm going to dream, dream big.

I never seriously took into consideration what my mom said. I always thought that because she was my mom, she was supposed to say things like that. However, as I've grown and matured in the last few years, I've seen how hard my mom has had it. I've also seen how strong those hard

MOTHER'S

Prose by Jacqueline Broeker, Senior

Tempera by Ashley Bloss, Senior

HELP

times have made her. As I went through some difficult times, I decided to confide in my mother and actually listen to what she had to say. We didn't agree on how to handle every situation, but I still wanted her advice. She was my rock and my stable support throughout those times, even when I knew she thought her world was falling apart.

This year is it. Graduation. It's the end to life as I know it now. It's a

beginning of a new chapter, a new book entirely. I am terrified, but I know that I will be all right. I have my mother's blood in me. I am strong. This writing is supposed to be about something I believe in, and that something is my mother. She is my hero, and I have her to thank for all that I've accomplished. Now in the mornings, I can get up with my alarm clock myself because I know everything's going to be ok.

Redemption by Abandonment

Drama by Jacob Ladyga, Senior
Watercolor by Allison Adkins, Junior

(Diane Bartlett walks slowly through the rain. The raindrops beat sporadically on her black umbrella as she works her way through the park. The shadow created by the clouds seems to deepen the greens of the trees, shrubbery, and grass around her. She drains the last drops of soda from her Pepsi can, tossing it into a trash can she passes. Her stained, purple T-shirt and torn blue jeans are marked by raindrops that evaded the umbrella. She leaves the confines of the park, walking over the bordering sidewalk and briskly traversing a city street to reach the row of buildings opposite. She lowers and closes her umbrella as she ducks into Kin's, a local bar.

The bar is slightly dingy, though relatively clean. She quickly scopes the room until she finds who she's looking for. A tall middle-aged man is sitting alone at a small table: Diane's soon to be ex-husband, Rhory Bartlett. She approaches him and takes the seat opposite as he looks up from his half-empty glass of beer.)
Rhory: (Smiling wistfully and whispering) Di, you came.
Diane:(In an exasperated, weary tone) Yes, Rhory, I came. But nothing's going to change. I told you that. I've listened to you a thousand times-
Rhory: Di, please! This is getting ridiculous! I'm different; you know that.
Diane: Shut up, Rhory. If this is why I'm here, you've just wasted more of my time. I've signed. Do the same and let me go.
Rhory: Diane, I've changed! I haven't touched a joint in weeks! I swear!
Diane: That's not it and you know it Rhory! What about the coke? You were so good at hiding all this from me before! Why should I believe you now? You promised me, Rhory! I said I would marry you if you stopped, and you couldn't even make it a year! How can you do that? How stupid can you possibly get? Have you ever thought what could happen to you if a dealer showed up at the apartment? What if I had been there? That's why I left you Rhory. You're stupid and you're selfish!
Rhory: Anna, I'm sorry. God, I'm so sorry. You're right. I was selfish, all right, I know. But that's over. Please come home! Your things are still at the apartment: your clothes, your books…and that antique Buddha your grandmother brought over from Vietnam. You can't leave that with me and you know it…Please, Anna?
(Diane silently looks at Rhory. Absentmindedly, she consents to the waitress filling up her coffee cup as she contemplates the uncharacteristically sincere expression on Rhory's face. Her expression softens as she lifts her coffee and sips it pensively. She places the cup back on the table.)
Diane: Rhory…you know I love you. But…
Rhory: Di…please? Just come back to the apartment. Please?
Diane: (Taking one last sip from her cup) All right, Rhor. Let's go.
(Diane and Rhory enter their second floor apartment on Bradson Avenue. It's a small but very well kept place. The Bartletts' adoration for Asian culture is evident, though blended well with modern

Western styles. The apartment had represented the perfect marriage of the girl from South Vietnam and the boy from rural Michigan. A perfection all but obliterated by reality. Diane and Rhory enter, taking seats across from one another at the small wooden table in their kitchen.)

Rhory: So…smell anything, Diane?

Diane:(Taking in a slow, controlled breath) Well, (chuckling slightly) for once I can actually smell the sandalwood. But you know, Rhory, coke has no sm-…

(There is a sharp knock at the door. Smiling, Rhory stands up and quickly moves to the door. He only manages to begin opening it before an elderly woman bursts in. She is wearing a typical flannel sun dress. Her bright silver hair is styled in tight curls. Her spectacles have thick burgundy frames, and the eyes behind them have a look of maternal ferocity.)

Old Woman: All right Mr. Bartlett, let's get this going.

(Without even pausing to look at Diane, the woman ransacks the Bartlett apartment. She looks under cushions, behind dressers, in cabinets, through closets, and even behind the toilet tank and the air vents. After nearly an hour of non-stop frantic searching, the woman comes and sits at the small wooden table where Diane had remained and Rhory had replaced himself after letting her in.)

Old Woman: Well, Rhory, another clean week. Congrats! That makes four. But you've still got a ways to go.

Rhory: I know, Elaine. Um, I don't think you've met my wife Diane?

Elaine: (Acknowledging Diane for the first time) Oh! So this is Mrs. Bartlett? You weren't lying Rhory. She's beautiful.

Diane: Thank you. Um, so how long have you known Rhory, Elaine?

Elaine: Dear, since he came into my apartment a week after you left. I live on the ground floor, you see, and one night I came home to find a rather pathetic-looking specimen on the floor by my door. Now, I'm typically foolishly accepting of strangers, and this man was weeping right at my feet. I asked him what was wrong. He told me he'd really screwed everything up. He told me about his beautiful wife and the promise he'd made her. He also told me how he selfishly broke that promise. I'd never seen a more broken and helpless person. After an evening of coffee and homemade cookies, Rhory and I made an agreement. Every other day I stop by here and turn this place upside down in exchange for a dinner every Sunday. Your husband is quite the chef. Regardless, dear, no matter what his shortfalls, he's never stopped loving you. If he stopped loving anyone, it was himself. Amor Vincit Omnia, right? He has been great these last few weeks. Not so much as an ounce of anything other than his cooking spices. He has changed, dear, and he misses you.

(Diane looks at Rhory, who has been silent thus far. They lock eyes, and he dares a smile. That smile is his. It is Rhory behind it. For the first time in a very long time, she sees the man she had married and still loves.)

Passion

Fiction by Ariel Beatty, Senior
Ink by Nicole Noland, Senior

Passion looks not in your eyes, but in your soul. She takes her hand and reaches to the very bottom, pulling your strongest feelings out in the open, clutching them in her hand. Passion takes your mind and shows you what it is like to be at the very height of your senses. She leads you to the one thing you want more than anything else in this world. Passion whispers lusts in your ear, making you want it that much more. She can smell your feelings and uses them to her advantage. She now has you in her power, and she grips you tighter and tighter until you finally release yourself, all of yourself, to her. Passion is the best feeling in the world.

Desire

Fiction by Dalynn Clingenpeel, Junior

Desire is a small child in a toy store with shifting eyes, scanning the building with a yearning for everything he wants, but can't have. He walks the aisles with mysterious wonder, touching everything in sight, for fear that it may not be real. Desire smells like fresh baked cookies and sweets that linger in the room while you're still waiting for dinner where green vegetables are sitting in front of you. While you wait ever so patiently for what you desire, the piercing look in his eyes mesmerizes as he draws you near. The feeling of his presence is warm, like coals glowing on a dying fire, yet you can feel him burning your heart. He reaches in and grabs with a force so strong, you can't focus your attention anywhere else. He has consumed you. All you think about is him. Even in your dreams, he taunts you, dangling himself right in front of you.

She Has

*Poetry by Mike
Morgan, Senior*

*Pastel by Brooke
Poeppel, Senior*

She has reds. Her lips are light and swollen with noise.
They soften with love. They soften with grace and subtle speech.
They are red and anything but fierce.

She has yellow. She holds it in thin whisks of her hair. They are so tempting,
Playing with my thoughts, playing with my eyes. Her yellow is always playing.

She has her blues. In the vibrant cotton She wears. How it plays with her dark skin!
It's hard for me to tell what is real and what is cloth. She looks so good in blue.

She has greens. They lay in the softest parts of her heart. As She lies in the green grass,
I see them as She tears at the stems and blades that lie around her. I see how bold
Of a green She longs for.

She has gold, silver, and platinum. She shows it through her skin, through her smile.
She shows it in her eyes. She is priceless. The riches of gold sit themselves in her soft skin,
The silver in the glisten of her eyes before we fall asleep, the platinum in her selfless soul.
Always trying to please me, make it up to me, She's made it up to me.
She has.

The Night My Angel Fell

Fiction by Jacob Ladyga, *Senior*
Ink by Allison Adkins, *Junior*

I had never felt as hopeless as I did that night. The ecstasy of the last three years felt like vague recollections from a previous life as I sat alone in the heart of my own personal hell. He and I had laughed at how poetic our story was: the beautiful love shared between an educator and an artist; an amorous tale about an English teacher and a ballet dancer. A beautiful dream…one I felt I hadn't deserved. And now one I feared to lose forever…

I caught a glimpse of my eyes on the metallic surface of the fork I was twirling in my right hand; my untouched tray of food sat on my lap. I had always had an appreciation of how startlingly green my irises became when my eyes were bloodshot. I stopped twirling the fork when another vision caught my attention; almost directly below my eye, a fresh cut extended nearly to my left earlobe. Suddenly, I felt a lump in my throat as the events of less than an hour ago flashed across my mind…

Josh and I were on our way out for the night. The Poet Laureate had a new book that was being released at the Barnes and Noble a few blocks from our apartment building. To commemorate the book's release, she was going to be at the bookstore signing the first copies. I kept telling Josh that I would just get it later, since he had a performance the next evening, and I didn't want him exhausted. Of course, he didn't listen.

"And what kind of husband would I be if I let you miss out on this?" he asked, thrusting his face within an inch of mine, molding it into that mock-serious expression that always made me laugh. It was unfair, really. His smile was so charming, and his dark brown eyes, so loving. My resolve never could hold up long against that combination.

Around eleven that night, we walked hand in hand out of our apartment building, opting for the more conventional doors just to the left of the building's new revolving door. Josh and I were at a loss to explain the utility of this new addition; perhaps some people were centripetally-inclined.

We walked down the street together, the ceaseless life of New York City enveloping us in a chaotic blend of light, sound, and vibration. We laughed quietly to ourselves as we reminisced about our wedding day less than a year ago. Josh and I had wanted an authentic gay wedding, albeit a small and intimate one. We, along with a small group of friends and family, traveled to a secluded pine forest in the heart of Vermont. There, under Nature's canopy, Josh and I pledged our souls to one another.

In all the metropolitan mayhem and blissful conversation, we could hardly be blamed for failing to hear them. Two burly strangers grabbed Josh from behind. Another pushed me to the ground, and I looked up to see a man with a shaved head and a gold nose ring that clashed horribly with his pale skin.

Before I could even begin to look for Josh, the man grabbed me by the hair and pulled me back into the mouth of an alley Josh and I had just crossed. Over my own moans of pain, I heard a shuffling and loud grunts from deeper in the alley.

I tried to stand up, but barely got to my knees before I felt a burning sensation across my face. I let out a cry of pain as I felt a stream of blood pour down my cheek and along my chin. Somewhere a few feet from me I could still hear the grunting and rapid shuffling. I looked up in the direction of the noise. My breath caught, and my eyes stung when I saw him. In the glow of a purple neon sign marking the entrance to some sleazy strip club, I saw Josh's tense and frightened face. The two men who had grabbed him on the street now held him pinned against the wall of the alley. The third man with the nose ring was now walking quickly towards them, the pocketknife in his hand stained with my blood.

He was in front of Josh before I knew what was happening. As I screamed and struggled to my feet, another scream joined mine. I blundered to the slumped form of my husband as our assailants fled down the other end of the alley, screaming, "Fags!" and laughing uproariously as they ran.

Josh dropped to the ground, blood seeping from his stomach as he moaned in agony. As I tried to get his arm around my shoulders, a group of construction workers walked out of the strip club, laughing obnoxiously and reeking of whiskey. They all stopped when they saw us. I hadn't even opened my mouth to speak before two of them helped Josh to his feet and another was on his phone calling for help...

Now here I was, sitting in the reception area of a hospital, with hope slipping from me. I stared blankly at a child who was showing great enthusiasm for the McDonald's Happy Meal her mother had just presented to her.

Suddenly, in that moment, an internal dam broke. My vision became blurry as I quickly looked down at my folded hands. The thin silver wedding band on my left ring finger was caked with blood. I neither knew nor cared whether the blood was mine or Josh's. He was my everything; if

he died, the only valuable part of my life, of myself, would go with him. I was suddenly jolted back to awareness by the sound of my name being called out, "Ian Grahm."

I jumped up and looked toward the operation room doors. A young African-American man in mint green scrubs was looking expectantly around the room. I moved in a determined yet tentative way until I was before him. As he looked at me, a smile spread across his youthful features.

"Great news," he said as I stood shaking slightly before him. "Josh did great. The knife missed all of the vital organs. There was considerable blood loss, but he'll be back to normal in a few days. Until then I would like to keep him here."

Relief washed over my entire body. Barely able to form the words, I asked in an almost inaudible voice, "Can I see him?"

"Of course. He's very tired, but you are more than welcome to see him," he replied,

a caring smile appearing on his youthful visage.

I followed him through the bland hallways of the hospital. It was a blur of beige walls and fluorescent lighting. Within a few minutes we stood before a dark green door with a brass plaque engraved with the number 629. He opened the door and held it to allow me in first. As I walked in and managed to take in the whole room, I felt pressure starting to build up in my chest again.

There he was, propped up on a pillow with a copy of Walden by Thoreau. He was wearing the black-rimmed, square spectacles I always loved to see on him. At the sound of our approach, he turned and looked right at me, the most gorgeous smile known to humanity breaking across his face when he saw me.

"Hey, honey," he said sweetly.

I walked slowly over to him until I was by his side; then I lost it again. The tears came and my knees buckled from under me. All the emotions identified on the human spectrum burst through me in a tempest of passion. I felt fear; fear that stemmed from the near loss of my husband and soulmate. I felt anger; anger towards all of those who wage war on a love they simply do not understand. However in this moment, relief held the most power. He was here, still, to love me and be loved by me. He was going to be fine. And in this moment, all else was lost to me but the man in my arms, the love of my life, the beat of my heart.

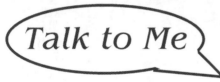
Talk to Me

Poetry by Cassie Philson, Senior
Ink by Amanda Bachtel, Sophomore

You talked to me and I talked to you.
You didn't talk to me and I didn't talk to you.
I don't know about you but I want to talk to you.
I see you and my heart goes wild.
Talk, Talk, Talk. No, No, No. Yes, Yes, Yes.
I'm sorry but I can't. Why? Because I'm too shy.
He talked to me but I blew it. I didn't pursue him
and he's not going to pursue me. He tried to talk to me
but I didn't follow through. I talk to him only when he talks
to me, which isn't as often now. Why? Because I don't talk.
You can't have a conversation with a mute. Eventually they
stop trying. Why do I do this? It's how I was made. How I was
raised, with insecurities. Always being put down. Never raised up.
Now I believe what they say so I don't talk. I don't know what to say.
I want to say something but nothing ever comes. So all I can do is
watch.. and wait... and maybe just maybe he will talk to me.

Waiting

Poetry by Lee Back, Senior
Charcoal by Brooke Poeppel, Senior

I saw you there, just a moment ago,
Wandering, waiting for me to say something,
But yet I would just stare.
What I thought I saw, I really didn't,
And what you thought I said, I knew I couldn't.
For the life of me I don't know why.

Love had passed us by in just that short moment of time
To leave us in puzzlement, wondering what could have been.
But as I look back upon what happened, I realize something-
You were always there at the oddest times,
And not realizing it at first, I was too late to recognize it.
For the soul of me I don't know why.

I felt as though everyone else had you,
But I was left to wander alone.
I searched for you high and low,
But I found that it didn't matter how hard I searched,
You couldn't be found.
I learned that you had to be felt from deep down inside.
For the heart of me I don't know why.

The years had passed, and the suns had set,
And as we aged, not a wrinkle on your face
Took away from your beauty.
What I thought was love was really lust
And what I thought was a friendship
Was the beginning of something so much more.
For the love of me I don't know why.

I wish someday to have the courage to say what I feel,
But until then we can still stay friends,
'Cause I feel the beginning of so much more.
I know that the best things in life are worth waiting for,
And you're worth so much more.
Love is my disease, yet it is also my cure.
This I know for sure!

[Beneath the Surface]

CONFESSIONS
of a
Farm Girl

Prose by Jackie Broeker, Senior

Living on a farm is rough, but being a girl on a farm is even worse. My dad has only my sister and I to help out, and I'm the oldest. I've always helped my dad. He calls me "Jack," his boy.

My dad has taught me well. Since we work together all the time, I've picked up a few tricks of the trade. For instance, work smarter not harder. I know relatively how most machinery works, and I've built muscle. It's not easy work.

My favorite time of the year is summer. It's also hay season. I love being outside cutting and raking the hay. Driving around in circles is surprisingly calming. I enjoy this time because I have time to think and I get a great tan. When that's all done, then the hard work begins. Bailing hay is not a two man (actually in this case, one man and one girl) job. It can be, but remember, work smarter not harder. So my dad calls guys he knows to help out. As I've gotten older, they've all been my boyfriends or guy friends. It has always annoyed me how those big, tough guys have treated me. They come to the field strutting their stuff in cut off sleeves and talking big. I would get so angry when they'd tell my dad to get better help. To them, I was too little, not strong enough, and to top it all off, I was a girl. My dad would just smile at them and then wink at me. By the end of the day, ten wagon loads or so later, we'd call it quits. At least one boy would've puked by then, and they were all exhausted. Nobody was poking fun at me now because I was the only one able to keep up with my dad. My dad would pat me on the back and say, "Come on, Jack. Let's go home. See you girls tomorrow." That one simple line would lift my spirits no matter how mad or exhausted I felt.

For ten years I've worked alongside my dad. We've had our good times and bad times, but we always get through it together. We've never had the same help two consecutive years in the hay field. They just can't seem to handle those 5-8 hours of hard work while my dad and I have been there all day. Now, when our help starts talking big at the beginning of the first cutting, my dad says, "Boys, there's enough hot air out here! Get to work." Then he looks at me with that proud look that any father has for his son and says, "Set the pace, Jack."

Where I Come From

Poetry by Ethan Marosz, Senior

I am from a backyard of dirt and weeds,
From a home and a neighborhood
Where there was more fear of gunshots and robbery
Than any make-believe monsters,
From a place where Popeye's chicken was the favorite dinner feast,
And it was mostly smoke for dessert.

I am from the spaceship playground
Built for the kid here before me
By the father there before mine.
I am from Amadeus and random hamsters,
My only long haired friends to speak with at times.

I am from an Academy of those above
My status, intelligence, and wealth,
From a place where price didn't affect decisions,
But look and status too often did.

I am from re-marriage,
From two single people trying at a family again.
I am from where that took place,
Hickville, USA, where your truck is your best friend.
From here, I found more than I ever thought could be found:
The women I pray to marry and a few of the best friends that the best has to offer.

I am from mistakes and disappointments,
From letdowns and shortcomings,
From lack of mind and loss of heart.

I am from somewhere, someone who is proud of me anyway,
Up in Heaven, a God who says I'm a good kid,
From love that surpasses everything else.

I am from Love.

What I Am

Poetry by Chloe Bugajski, Senior
Charcoal by Chloe Bugajski, Senior

Place of Birth
In the arms of a
loved one, covered
with warmth.
I was tired after
winning the great
race in Kansas City, Missouri.

Ethnic Origin
We're all the same.
I am me. You are you. He is he.
No difference, only opinions.
I am white. Black. Red. Yellow.
Now, tell me,
do you know what you are?

Religion
God gave me life,
not a big bang,
and I absolutely did not
evolve from any ape.
I will go to Heaven,
not because I am good,
but because I believe.

Career Goal
I erase.
I paint with my hands.
I smudge my pencil.
I shoot people,
as well as nature.
I'm an artist, making myself.

HOMELESS ANGEL

Fiction by Mike Morgan, Senior
Photo by Hannah Hummel, Senior

He took the transit every morning to God knows where. You could see he clearly didn't have a job. But every day he sat there at the back of the bus. He was a corroded, old man. No expression. An eyesore with long, scraggily, gray hair that was darker than usual due to a lack of hygiene. His face was swollen with a long, white beard with equal patches of dark musty browns and

faded blacks. His dark, sun-tarnished skin was covered from head to toe in a fine dusty powder. His trench coat long and worn barely held its original tan color. It was painted with oil and dirt. Its edges were frayed and dragging on the floor. This gave way to his dirty, old fisherman boots. He was a man of decay. He sat there every morning with a cup of coffee from a machine. He clearly panhandled for this, as I'm sure he did for everything he owned.

It made me sick, this man with a blank expression. He was worthless. He contributed nothing to society. He didn't exist; perhaps it would be better if he really didn't. I'm usually not this bleak, but it upset me. He shared the same bus with me but none of the same morals, none of the work ethic. It disgusted me.

I resolved to pick up my briefcase and leave the bus a stop earlier that day. Whitmore Avenue was only three extra blocks away from my usual stop. The man proceeded to follow me off the bus. It made me nervous. He followed me a little ways down the block as we passed four shops or so. I began to grow anxious. The man continued to follow me.

My steps became heavier and quicker. He was still there behind me. I walked a little further until I could not take it anymore. I turned around in a blind rage and began to yell at the man. I was caught off guard when he dove after me. This was it. He was attacking me. I was being attacked. Or was I?

I hit the ground with a hard thump. I was awash with white for a few seconds, four or five at the most. I stood up to the sound of car horns and a gasping audience. The man, as I saw him, was on the ground face down, a little ways away from the dark red Mercedes. The car was smoking, and the window was cracked.

"Oh my God, that man...he saved you! Are you okay?" said a stranger from the crowd as he rushed to me.

"I, I,...I'm okay. He did save me." It was a sharp truth to realize, but this corroded man, this man I saw as useless, had just saved my life. God knows, he was my angel.

[Beneath the Surface]   105

Throwing Rocks

Fiction by Emily Thomas, Sophomore

Charcoal by Jeanna Hathaway, Sophomore

I can remember it so well. It's like this song was on repeat in my head and I couldn't turn down the music. That was the summer when everything changed. I can see it so clearly.

"Come on! We're almost to Willo's Fridge!" I called to my comrades.

"Why exactly do they call it Willo's Fridge anyway?" laughed Cara-mae.

"You never heard that story?" cried Carolina. "It's about that old guy, Roy Taylor. You see he had a pet raccoon that he got from a bet he won down in Arkansas. Well, Roy named that thing Willo, and one night Willo ran off. Poor Roy was stricken with grief that he threw his barn fridge down the ditch over there as a memorial!"

"Crazy old coot!" I yelled. My friends and I were almost to Robin's Ditch. It was a tradition that the three of us had started three years prior. Cara-mae, Carolina, and I, Claire, would ride our rusty, scarlet bikes down the dirt road to a clear little creek near a forgotten oak tree. The wisteria was in full bloom, and the water was so pristine that you could see the shallow, tawny creek bed. It was our summer place where we gathered to spend time together. This would be the last summer.

"Oh Clarie, why did you bring that hunky guitar? You know your daddy's going to kill you for having that in public view. I have too much to carry now, and my balance is horrific unlike some!" cried Cara-mae. My mother and father were a lawyer and a doctor respectively. They lived in a place where everything was either black or gray and no color was allowed. I was a big purple splotch on their checkerboard lives. When I was young, my grandma gave me her guitar from her dancing days. The polished wood was faded, and the fret board had tiny sterling silver birds flying between the strings.

"Here, Clarie dear. This will help you run away from things for a bit when you need it. This guitar can take you places. Trust it, love," she would say. I really loved my grandma. I got my balance from her. I have been known to ride a bike and eat a bag of Cheeto's at the same time with no trouble at all. It's a gift.

"Are we there yet?" called Carolina.

"Oh, you're not giving up yet! It's right there, my impatient little friends," I cried back. We parked our bikes and set up the kick stands. We made our way down to the edge of the water, setting our backpacks down by the bank.

"Oh I love it here," said Carolina. "I'm really going to miss this place."

I got out the Sharpies, brilliant colored pens for our scripted wishes. "Yeah, senior year of high school's done with, life's nearly over," I replied sarcastically.

"I'm serious guys! In a few days I'm going to be halfway across the world! I don't know how I'm going to deal!" cried Carolina solemnly. Carolina Newland was going to spend the next few years in Italy with her cousin Stella. Carrie was going to live in Milan and hopefully get a job as an actress for one of those Italian soap operas, Le Bella Vive, The Pretty Life. Carolina was perfect for a soap. She had deep brown hair, olive skin and eyes closest to the color of dark-washed blue jeans.

"At least you can leave this place," I said. "You can see a little bit more of the world than I will. You will be able to see past Williamson, Tennessee, with all the cornfields and front porches. Take it as a journey."

"I'm leaving, too. I hate to leave, but it's what I have to do," added Cara-mae. "College and then marriage! At the time I need you two the most, I will be miles away!" What Cara said was true. She was going to a college way up north in Indiana or Michigan. Notre something. After she graduated, Cara and Austin were going to get hitched. The first time I saw Austin Hughes, I thought he was socially retarded or something. He had a huge metal helmet thing over his head because, I later found out, he got in a bad truck accident. It messed up his jaw, so he had to wear the headgear for three months. I'm not saying that Austin looked terrible, because underneath the metal was a sweet face, blue eyes and brunette hair that fell over one eye. Metal Mouth was gorgeous; it was just that I only saw the surface of him on the first day. After his jaw healed, Cara-mae and Austin were always together. They fit together perfectly. Cara was short and stubborn and very opinionated. Austin loved that about Cara. A date was set for a spring wedding.

"Okay, enough about your future lives!" I proclaimed as I strummed my guitar. "Let's make our wishes, girls." I set down my beauty and grabbed a vermilion Sharpie. It was time for the tradition of throwing rocks into the tranquil water with our wishes tied on like a ribbon. We started this when we were freshmen, scared and innocent. It was a novel idea to cast out your wishes, as though that would help them to come true. We simply wrote a few words on a nearby stone, kissed it and tossed it out to the creek.

On one of my rocks I wrote "friendship." I kissed the smooth rock and tossed it out into the water. It made sapphire ripples in the still water. "For friends," I said.

Cara-mae piped, "For new things." Plunk.

"To a journey," called Carolina. Splash.

"For Austin," said Cara as she wrote the words in a curly script. Kiss. Whoosh. Splash.

"For Italy." Whoosh.

"For music."

On and on it went, our wishes for our newborn lives floating up into the azure sky as they sank into the heart of the creek. Maybe they would become possibilities.

"For... For being unique and different from my family," I declared. I turned to my friends as I threw my rock. "Cara, Carolina, tonight is the night for new things. I have a gig upstate, and my parents don't want me to go. They go on and on about how I should pursue some real job like a doctor or a lawyer. But they don't know what I want. I want to see the world and I want to perform, telling stories with my music. There is going to be a guy from Big Mountain Music, and if all goes well, I will have a record deal. I want my best friends to come with me." Cara-mae and Carolina stared back at me, their eyes pondering.

"We will be front and center," said Cara-mae.

"You should do what you need to do for yourself. Music makes you happy. Stay with it," added Carolina.

"My opening song is for you guys," I said smiling. I scribbled the word "Luck" on a new rock and threw it forcefully.

That was the summer I made my first million. "Throwing Rocks" made the nation's top ten list within a month of my deal. My parents eventually

accepted the fact that I was not going to become a politician, and they were proud of my accomplishments. I guess they just wanted the best for me. After all the fights and arguments, and the applications to Harvard and Yale that I refused to send, all the time I spent with my grandmother's guitar finally made them realize that I had a different life to lead.

I guess it sounds pretty corny: "Okay, so a seventeen year old Southern bombshell gets it all." Maybe it was my perseverance or my friendship with Cara-mae and Carolina that helped me through. By the way, Cara-mae got married to Austin, and they are expecting children. They are very excited. Carolina is living in Italy but she didn't get the job, so maybe she will come back to the states soon.

It could've been the rocks as well. I dedicated my first album to Cara, Carolina, Robins Ditch, and the summer that everything changed. Kiss. Swoosh. Splash.

All I Really Want Is You

Poetry by Cassie Philson, Senior
Ink by Brooke Poeppel, Senior

I see your face when I close my eyes
You are a beauty in every way
I really want you and I don't know why

I dream of you when I lie
One was of you on the bay
I see your face when I close my eyes

I can't stop no matter how I try
I want you but I can't make you stay
I really want you and I don't know why

If only I could fly
I would go to you if I may
I see your face when I close my eyes

I never want to say goodbye
I would be in such dismay
I really want you and I don't know why

Wanting you is making me cry
'Cause I can't be with you, not today
I see your face when I close my eyes

I really want you and I don't know why

Under the Stars

Poetry by Phil VanWanzeele, Senior

Under the stars the moon kisses my cheek.
As you softly kiss my lips,
The wind's breath tickles the leaves
As mine tickles your ear whispering, "I Love You."
The night sky shines so sweetly
As our hearts beat in unison.
I could lay here sewn in her arms forever
Looking up at our sparkling, violet blanket.
There are billions of stars staring in my eyes
But none are as beautiful as the one to my right,
The only star in my sky. . .

Only a Reflection

Poetry by Emily Jaske, Junior
Watercolor by Kate Smith, Junior

I watch you sail off into the sunset.
You say just to explore the new land;
I say to explore new love.
The scene is bittersweet.
You sail off with what you say are good intentions
But your white sail won't be white for long.
So leave-
Just leave me here, a reflection of the broken
rocks
And waves,
Tears burning the backs of my eyes like
The sun to the sky,
But know you don't have my heart.
You only had a reflection of what my
Love is like.

Words Left (Unsaid)

Fiction by Phil VanWanzeele, Senior
Tempera by Olivia Hurley, Sophomore

There comes a time in everyone's life when it is time to die. In some cases, the person who dies is young, and these incidents seem even more tragic because the person seemingly had years to live. This is a story of two such people.

Maria was a naturally beautiful woman. She didn't need any make-up, and she didn't care enough in the first place to wear any. Being a single mother with two young children, how could she have time? At nineteen, she was married and a homemaker. By twenty-seven she was a widow and was working two jobs to scrape by.

She was born near the Buffalo Bayou in Texas and throughout her life worked her way northeast to Missouri. Her mother died when she was young, and her father, being a trucker, wasn't home very much. As a result, she moved in with her mother's mother on a little farm in Pinola County. Over the next two years, her father's visits grew few and far between until they eventually became nonexistent. A year passed after her father's last visit, and her grandmother died on Easter Day, leaving her alone again. At the age of seven, with no one close to take care of her or at least close who cared for her, she moved to her Auntie Lynne's in McAlester, Oklahoma. Auntie Lynne was her mother's older sister and was a single school teacher in the McAlester Public School Corporation. Not surprisingly, she stressed education. The girl who had encountered nothing but change finally had some normalcy in her life. She stayed in McAlester until she graduated from McAlester High School at the top of her class.

She met Benjamin in college at the University of Oklahoma. He was from Missouri, and less than a year after graduation, they were married. Ironically, the two moved to Ben's home town of Houston, Missouri, in Texas County. They had two children in their marriage, and life was good. They lived happily together until Ben, who was in seemingly good health, suddenly had a stroke and died while on a business trip.

Tuesday's were homemade pizza night. On Tuesdays she worked the third shift and got off work at quarter till eight. Routinely, she went to the grocery store to get the week's groceries, including those for the homemade pizza on Tuesday nights.

As she pulled out of the grocer's parking lot, her vehicle was blindsided by a drunk driver who failed to turn on his lights before leaving The Mole Hole Tavern four miles up the road. Her green, Ford Pinto collapsed like a coke can under the force of the drunk driver's truck. Fearing arrest, he fled, leaving her bleeding and unconscious, prepared to meet her maker. When the ambulance arrived, she was lying in a lake of blood with countless lacerations upon her face and head. The rescuers attempted to use the Jaws of Life, but the vehicle was completely crushed. Time was running out for her due to the steady stream of gasoline leaking from the Pinto near the flames shooting from the crushed hood. Firefighters pulled her out, risking the loss of her legs. They were successful, although she hadn't regained consciousness.

Her mind was in a fog as she was hooked to every IV her body could stand. She couldn't speak to tell them where it hurt; she couldn't move to better suit her needs, so she slowly slipped back into a coma. Her two poor children would go without pizza that Tuesday night.

Upon arriving at the hospital, she slipped into an accident induced coma. Although she was completely awake, her eyes were closed and she was unable to move. She was aware of what they were doing, but she couldn't stop them as they began to investigate the cuts and bumps on her skull. Her children were called to her bedside where they began to weep. Soft tears started rolling down their cheeks onto their mother as they prayed for her survival. She felt the warm drops sitting in silent puddles upon her arm, and she recollected a dream of Benjamin.

They were going out that night. She looked absolutely stunning in her red dress, almost as if she were a fresh cherry innocently plucked from the tree. Ben stood a towering 6'5" but was a dwarf at the sight of her. His dishwater blond hair was gelled in a porcupine mess. His green eyes followed her body up and down, and he nearly fell to his knees. She hadn't been this "dolled up" since the wedding. Ben took a quick shot of whiskey to regain himself, grabbed the keys to their 1999 Chevy Impala SUV, and they were on their way to meet Beth and James at the Eagle's Nest Bar. That night, they both got so disastrously drunk that James took them home. They got into a fight over another guy she spent her time with most of evening. Ben was the jealous sort and didn't want anyone messing with "his girl." She slapped him for being so ridiculous, and he slept in the car that night. She washed the dishes with her warm tears the next morning and offered to make him eggs before he

left for his business trip. He politely declined, but on the inside, he was screaming with regret. He grabbed a bagel and left for the airport en route to Arizona. They kissed softly one last time, although they didn't know that, and said their goodbyes without a single, "I Love You." The alcohol he drank from the night before triggered a lapse in his cerebral cortex, cutting off blood flow to his brain, and causing the stroke. She was a wreck inside and out Completely lost without Ben and struggling to provide for the kids, she began to take prescription drugs to cope with the pain. She became plagued with "what ifs" and "whys" when there was no satisfactory explanation.

The lines distinguishing the hospital lights from the white light of paradise slowly began to gray and fade away. She slowly let go. The rich beat of her heart quieted. Her breath turned into a vague mist as the children watched in quiet awe. They became worried their mother would soon be gone, and they were right. At 11:06 p.m., Maria Rose Wells was pronounced dead from massive injuries caused by the accident, but what really killed her was a broken heart.

She was led into the light, not by a man with long flowing hair and scars in his palms, but by a gorgeous, blond haired man with recognizable features. She kissed Ben again for the first time. "I love you," they each said quietly to the other. Smiling happily, they each realized it was something they wanted to say since that day a long time ago.

Bee-Bop a Lou-La

I closed my eyes, and a smile lit up across my face, like candles in domino formation, spreading either direction. "Bee-Bop a Lou-La" softened in my ears as my grandma Dixie sang to me with her humorous character fixed in her face, filling me with familiarity. I rocked back and forth, keeping the rhythm with dancing imagination in my eyes as I closed and opened them, catching glimpses of her. "She's my baby," she continued, repeating it with an even smile from under her tiny, Irish button-nose. Her round face, with eyes creasing at the corners, allowed small lines to crack and travel to the distant parts of her face. Her simple, calming features held a light inside me as I watched her dark hair stay in place, nestled on top of her head.

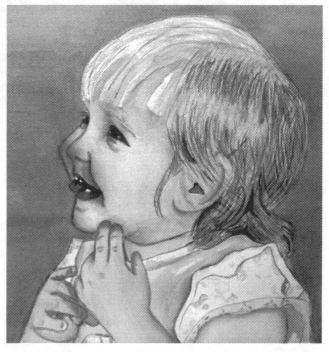

Prose by Kayleigh McMichael, Senior

Watercolor by Alysha Six, Senior

I cannot remember my age. There is only her and the music she hummed, which I stored within me like a waking lullaby. The room was warm, and the buzz of the television ricocheted about in the background. I sat squatted on a footstool in front of her, my usual spot when we would pat out "Pea Porridge Hot" on our legs and each others' hands, over and over again.

"Bee-Bop a Lou-La." She sang the same words, the only words for what I can recall. Furniture moved and changed as the years hung over Grandma Dixie's, or "Ma Dickie's" as I've called her since I was first beginning to talk. The stool stayed by the wooden stand next to the couch, clinging to a lamp atop its surface. She sang to me even when the green tint in my eyes began to film with exhaustion, eyelashes fluttering anxiously, careful not to drift asleep.

"Bee-bop a lou-la, she's my baby...."

David

Prose by Hannah Hummel, Senior
Charcoal by Seth Baker, Sophomore

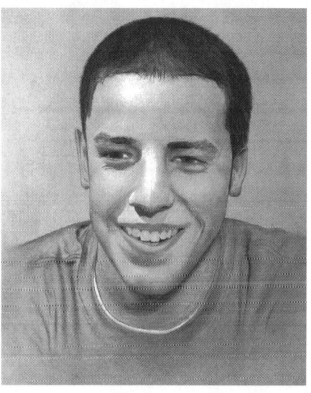

*W*ho knows? Maybe he's a real jerk, but I don't think so. He just seems too damn nice. He's the type of person who doesn't seem to talk much, but then again a lot of people think the same about me until they know me, so maybe I'm wrong about him. He's pretty good looking; I'd date him. Young, maybe twenty-one, twenty-two, he's got one of those thin faces. You know, the type where you can see that sharp, defined, sort of half square on each side of his face where his cheek bones are and the sides of his mouth. Some girls don't like guys who are skinny; I think it's pretty sexy. He's pretty thin all around, like he hasn't taken the time to sit down and enjoy a good meal in at least five years. His jacket has his name written on it; perhaps he works some blue collar job in a factory somewhere, tool and dye or something. He actually reminds me a bit of actor Christian Bale in The Machinist: quiet, lonely, just a little less crazy, I hope. His hands are never dirty though; I like that. Most of the guys who work in places like that have dark, greasy stains on their hands. His hands are clean, and he's got these long, thin, knobby fingers. Small, stylish glasses frame his big blue eyes that give him a sort of adorable, sad, puppy dog look. His hair is cut short. I usually don't like short hair, but it looks good on him. Besides, he looks like his hair would be ridiculously curly and uncontrollable if it was longer.

Every time he comes into the store, my heart beats a little faster. I feel like I should say something to him other than the usual, "Hi," and, "Have a nice night," but the next thing I know, he's got his Camel menthol cigarettes, swipes his credit card and he's gone. I should say something to him... maybe next time.

I Am a Machine

Poetry by Javier Galvez, Senior
Scratchboard by Kayleigh McMichael,
Senior

I am a machine
If you choose to keep reading, you'll know what I mean
I reach my destination
I feel this temptation
The pain consumes me inside
I need my music and somewhere to hide
The smile is only an act
I am useless and I accept this fact
I need to be taken away
To get lost, to become a stray
No flowers or sunshine for me
There's no love like there's supposed to be
I am a machine of love
You laugh, you mock, and you think you're above
I am however a machine
I run on love, not gasoline
I excrete it, I need it
My dials seem to be wrong however
Because my incoming love is taking forever
More and more is given away
Less is consumed than is needed to stay
You understand my pain
Why must you make me feel worthless, like life's in vain
Negative alternatives temporarily fuel my components
I need more love, more friends, less opponents
I am a machine and I need my fuel; I need love

First Kiss

Prose by Adam Kickbush, Freshman
Charcoal by Ashley Navilliat, Junior

I was 13 years old and in the 7th grade. One of my friends had invited me to a seemingly legendary party at her house. There were only about eight of us, and we were all close friends, so there was no risk of any drama occurring. We were all unimaginably excited at the fact that we would have six hours

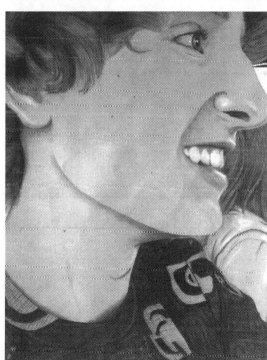

to hang out together without any unwanted interruptions. I was especially excited because there was a particular person there whom I wanted to see. I made sure I brushed my teeth extra thoroughly and rinsed my mouth out with mouthwash, just for good measure.

My best friend, Tom Sobieck, asked his sister to give us a ride to the party. We ended up passing the house, which was clearly visible from the street, three times before we successfully were in the driveway. My friend's house was rather large and white. She had a carpeted basement decked out with rope lights, couches, sofas, a big-screen T.V., and a ping-pong table that doubled as a pool table. I was amazed that anyone could own a space so superb.

I was ecstatic when I saw her there. She was the girl who made my world go round. The young woman who could make all the bad go away simply by existing. My girlfriend. As the party went on, we decided to go for a walk in the woods. Thinking ahead, I quickly slipped a Jolly Rancher candy in my mouth.

My friend had an incredible amount of land, much of which was covered in forest, a small area of grass, and the rest with small, soon-to-be Christmas trees. I was young and excited to just hold my girlfriend's hand. As we walked down the sandy pathway to the woods, I felt instantly at peace. I always had a passion for the woods, and with the added presence of my girl, I was in heaven. There was only one thing that could possibly make that night any better.

As the rest of the group moved on, my girlfriend and I slowed down and separated ourselves from them. She and I, alone at last. I knew exactly what I wanted, and this was the perfect day and time to do it. It was as if Mother Nature had set it up especially for me. The sun was setting, leaving a breathtaking sunset; the fireflies were carelessly flying around lighting up to each other; the coming night was giving us the perfect temperature, and there was a single tree on a dirt road next to a corn field. I knew this was the place and time, but I was too nervous and scared I would somehow mess up. That was when she asked me the question I had been waiting for: "How do you feel about kissing?"

"I feel great about it."
"Really?"
That was all I needed. As we approached the tree, we slowly faced each other. We took a moment to take in the quiet, soothing sound of the cicadas, puckered our lips, and leaned forward.

I will always remember my first kiss.

Mirror of the Mind
beneath the surface

"Some will not recognize the truthfulness of my mirror. Let them remember that I am not here to reflect the surface...but must penetrate inside. My mirror probes down to the heart. I write words on the forehead and around the corners of the mouth. Mu human faces are truer than the real ones."

- Paul Klee

Photo by Kayleigh McMichael, Senior

Loneliness, depression, and isolation lie hidden in the secret corners of the mind. Strip off the mask, the veil of deceit, the mirror's reflection to experience the heartache and tears just beneath the surface. Appearance and reality tease and torment both the observer and the observed. Dissect the mask, peel away the scars that cover truth and face the **mirror of the mind**.

Inanimate Object

Poetry by Kate Jenkins, Junior
Photo by Hannah Hummel, Senior

It's not a good day; that much is certain.
The ice on my windshield never thawed.
He held me... but it didn't last.
These things never do.
As I shut the car door,
    drive home in silence,
    trip up the stairs,
I can't shake this feeling, this idea,
That life is nothing but a revolving door
Void of an exit.
Then I see you.
Your condescending exactness is both uncalled for and unavoidable.
It is only you, Mirror, that never bothers with the white lies
And unanswered questions that come so easily to everyone else.
Solely the truth - no fabrications.
At first, I'm surprised... even offended by your bluntness.
But gradually, the more I stare into you,
The more I gain, the more I know.
Appreciation softens the edges.
I smile as I think of the words to say...
I guess I want to thank you for always telling the truth,
But instead, I stand in silence.
Talking to an inanimate object is a bit strange.

Fiction by Kate Jenkins, Junior
Scholastic Writing Award Certificate of Merit
Pastel by Brooke Poeppel, Senior

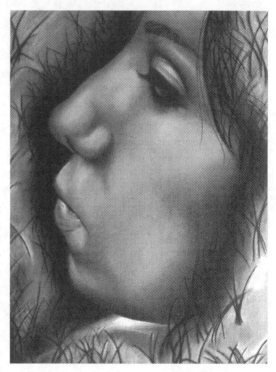

Sadness cannot look up. Her eyes are always locked at a point just ahead of her, never wavering. The ever present lump in her throat threatens to explode in a burst of blue and yellow if approached or bothered. She never speaks. A blistering, hot summer day spent at the beach one too many seasons ago was the last time her sing-song voice was heard. But everything changes; no one can be a child forever.

Sadness waits to shed tears until she is isolated; running along railroad tracks, chasing a place where no one will ever find her, like a metal plated box that captures all sound before it has a chance to echo through the outside world, arousing concerned parents and therapists. She lets her tears fall into plastic bags, then buries them in deserted fields. As she digs these holes, the menacing voice in her head screams, "All problems are best kept in the empty space between happiness and help. You need no one in this world but me."

She shivers as night descends on the small town she can never call home. Feeling nothing can be resolved in this life, she continues her walk to nowhere in particular.

Maroon

Poetry by Kayleigh McMichael, Senior

Maroon is tradition.
It is a bedside blanket, folded
And draped for future use.
It is the wrong shade of black,
The border of the night.
Maroon is her sweater in the
Fall, when her leaves undress the
Sky and shadow the wind.
It is the glare of the four a.m. sun
Onto the grass, damp with humid breath.
Maroon is your limbs, the coast,
The empty chair beside you,
The dark bedroom stutter.
It is the taste on your tongue,
The cold between the sheets.

The Truth

Poetry by Kate Jenkins, Junior
Charcoal by Ashley Navilliat, Junior

The truth is obscene
But wondering is worse,
Just say what you mean.

We hide behind a screen,
In lies, we immerse
Because the truth is obscene.

I have no need for caffeine,
My paranoia is a curse,
Just say what you mean.

Finally, you break the routine
Saying lines you rehearse
But you say what you mean.

I stare into you; your eyes are green,
Yet you place my heart in a hearse.
Yes, the truth is obscene but
Always say what you mean.

Endangered

Poetry by Kate Jenkins
Tempera by Amanda Bachtel, Sophomore

Running through smoke stacks,
Inhaling the fumes,
I chase you, young antelope,
But it's us both who are doomed.

I sprint to chase you,
My food, my desire,
But suddenly I stop,
Tripping on wire.

Our home is here somewhere,
A little less green,
A lot more dirty,
As I survey the scene.

Where are the trees
That were once so tall?
Replaced by a freeway
And a sturdy brick wall.

The air is not fresh,
The river not clear.
I am known for my speed
But I'm sluggish with fear.

I know we are rivals,
Predator and prey,
But together live in a place
That will be gone someday.

We are endangered,
Soon to be destroyed.
Say goodbye to the life
Our kind once enjoyed.

Ocean Blue

Poetry by Virginia Castro, Senior
Oil by Alysha Six, Senior

The mysteriousness of cool, dark water
can engulf a man rather quickly.
Red coral reefs, yellow fluttering flounder
attract me towards the heart of the ocean.
If I could, I would swim endlessly and never come
up for air. My goodness, air! I wonder how much
of it remains in my tank.
A liter. Just enough for one last deep breath!
How could I allow myself to forget the outside
world and lose myself in this deep dark ocean?
I came to you blue, to escape the chaos that occurs in
the world above us. You are unlike the sun who has a
beam of light constantly shining down at me, revealing
what I am. A lurking monster. Ocean, you capture me,
wash away my scars and cuts, cleanse me, make me new.
My lungs fill up with water as I gasp for you to save me
from my troubles. I wriggle forward and back desperately.
Your snakelike seaweed tangles all around me, pulling and tugging
my body. My eyes start to roll back, and I remember now how she
willingly gave herself to me, just as I have given myself to you.
I trapped her and laughed at her as she took her last breath,
her eyes crying for me to come rescue her.
Ocean blue, please stop laughing.

Melancholy

Fiction by Jacob Ladyga, Senior

Melancholy is a tall, willowy woman with obsidian hair. Her grace is comparable to a leaf in a gentle autumn breeze. She gazes into your soul with arctic blue eyes lined by full midnight lashes. She will charm you with her chime-like laughter. Her sable silk dress wisps across the floor as she looms about you. The sweet ring of her siren's voice curdles your blood like the venom of a serpent. Once under her spell, you will, too late, realize your folly. She will sting you with her visions of gloom. Her laughter will turn to a cackle of scorn. Her beauty will fade into the visage of the demons now haunting your present. The black silk of her gown will swell until you are obscured in its oblivion. The light of your life will be shrouded in cruel Melancholy's soulless abyss.

Scratchboard by Nekodah Niedbalski, Senior

Her

Prose by Avalon Minker, Senior
Colored Pencil Amber Zoellner,
Senior

Every morning after waking up, the first thing I do is put my mask on. I walk around all day with my mask on. Everyone thinks I have it good. No one sees what is under my mask. I am a good actress; I put my mask on, and I become my character. Few can see through the mask; many don't want to. When talking to people, I am not myself. I am my character. People say they are my friends. They are not friends with me; they are friends with her, my character. She is always trying to make everyone happy. She wants to be on top; myself, on the other hand, I have given up.

When you hit the bottom, why try to get back up? Isn't it easier to stay where you are? I have found it much easier to just be someone else and not be myself. I

like her better; everyone likes her better. She has almost completely taken me over. Few traits you see are me. She dresses like all the popular kids, Hollister head to toe. Myself, on the other hand, I would rather wear sweat pants and a t-shirt everyday. She coats her face with make-up; I would never bother to try. Why do I do this, I sit and ask myself? I want to have friends; I want to be happy; and I just want to fit in.

I do not fit in. I haven't for a few months now. It wasn't my fault. All the people in my town have shunned me. They see me and turn away, as if their eyes burn in horror. The friends I once had hate me; they talk behind my back. I wish that I could speak up and tell them all the truth, but my voice hides inside me. My voice is not the same now; it is weak and strongly soiled. I try and try, but it will not come out. It, too, hides behind her. My community thinks I've betrayed them, when really it was not a choice. They would all truly know if I could use my voice.

It has been a long two years, but when I leave here, I will be myself again. I will not need them. I will break free from her grasp and be alive again. She will not be my master; I will rule once again. I will walk away, never to return. Free and on the road, I will be myself. I will find a place to live my life and love myself once again.

She

Poetry by Lindsey Houston, Junior
Colored Pencil by Ashley Navilliat, Junior

She is cute,
But worth nothing.
She is smart,
But never gets A's.
She has deep blue eyes,
But everyone looks past.
She is hurting,
But no one cares.
She has scars
But shows only her blade.
She is damaged,
But no one has the glue.
One day she will be free,
Free from the world.
No one to judge.
No one to judge.
Only her and her orange bottle of white little regrets.
Only she decides how many it will take
To leave her body entirely,
To be free from it all,
To get away from it all.
Only her and her plan.
No one to change her mind,
Only her choice
Till she falls to the deep.

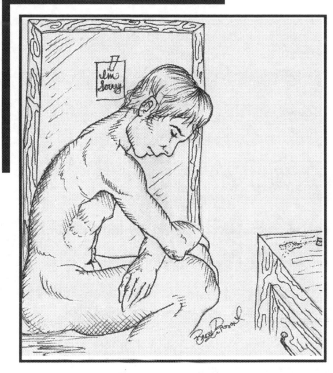

I Gave It Up

Poetry by Kayleigh McMichael, Senior
Ink by Brooke Poeppel, Senior

"I gave it up...once."
It rarely got much further than that.
They expected more from me, and I
knew it.
I strangled every attempt to do the
expected thing.
"I tried," was a typical claim straight
from my weak tongue.
Then again, is it considered "weak"
    when it's more of a refusal?
But you receive only one question:
    What does it mean to exist?
The irony is that the answer isn't
anywhere near positive.
I sat in those meetings, following the
steps and straightening my tie.

You nod, you go home, you open the box.
It never failed.
She'd sit on the sofa, her palms clutching one another, as if trying to catch
Her wavering emotions the way a child swings a butterfly net,
Reaching to capture that perfect creation of God.
I cheated every night with that beautiful stretch of powder.
Hope had lapped me a few times by now and she knew it.
Still, she dropped me off at that hollow brick building ever Thursday.
She'd kiss my cheek in a way that I could feel her praying internally.
One hour a week was supposed to change my life;
It changed hers.
I mumbled conversations around myself and made the notion to change,
But before the conversation was over, the box had let me in again.
I would roll over and let the ringing drain from my ears.
Scotch tape on a molding mirror held a piece of paper that clenched to her perfume,
With blue ink tracing the words "I'm sorry."
She could see right through me; we both knew it.
Now, a more empty box in a more lifeless house.
Thursdays come and go.
I walk to that hollow brick building, eyes dart
Blank across the room.
I nod, straighten my tie, and grip her note in my hand.
My heart stutters as I look for words to pull me through.
"I gave it up once, I gave her up once...,"

LO Keys NELY

Fiction by Kayleigh McMichael, Senior

Watercolor by Kate Smith, Junior

Her hand calmly tosses back the willowy brown hair twisting like a vineyard in front of her face. The burning whites of her eyes swarm over the cafe like Mormon rain. Lips weep over a microphone while the voice

behind them spills as if it were a sweet chardonnay, buried in a cemetery of ripened anxiety. A sustained pedal under her foot meets the floor with silent expiration as it draws the notes of the keys out beyond the walls each time her fingers gallop across them. Two men at the bar, dateless and lacking sobriety, appear to be speaking in tongues from her distant view while watching her take notice of them. Her eyes reject the sky and reach for a neon sign across the street. She slips off the bench, her arms stretching to find the sleeves of her jacket. The chilly cuff link buttons awaken her wrists. She pushes open the door as the yawning bell above it jingles a solemn "goodnight."

Regret

Fictions by Kelsey Piotrowicz, Junior
Watercolor by Brooke Poeppel, Senior

Regret dances with Memory to a tune from the past. As he glides across the floor, he hums along and sings the familiar lyrics- the words you never got a chance to say. Your conscience is his instrument. Like a gentleman, Regret opens the door to give you a glimpse of what could have been. Being a courteous man by nature, he never lets you forget the mistakes that were made or the experiences you didn't have. Regret is a wonderful partner, never letting you out of his embrace. How lucky we are to have Regret to catch us if we fall.

Deception is seen only by those who desire to find her. Her charming mask and ornate clothes disguise the horror behind the facade. She whispers her secrets and spreads her lies by the grace of her unfailing tongue. By the sound of her angelic voice, her songs are cleverly sung. Truth is enveloped in her frigid fingertips and tucked away until she's ready to set it free. Like a caged bird, truth waits. Guilt is her only enemy and chases her down every path she takes. She escapes rarely unscathed, only to continue her journey to someone else's heart. Deception drags the truth chained to her side, betrayal following close behind.

Deception

CONTROL

Prose by Nicole Noland, Senior
Scholastic Writing Award Gold Key Winner
Watercolor by Nicole Noland, Senior

Whenever I think back to when I was In Control, you always look the same. Blonde hair pulled back in a ponytail, tied with a red ribbon. Your bare legs were sticking out of a black cheerleading uniform you pretended to have a love-hate relationship with. Truth was, you really didn't mind wearing the god-forsaken thing, polyester and all. It was the only thing that made you feel connected to the other cheerleaders. Like a part of a group. Accepted. You'd broken out into a cold sweat, partly from the brisk October night, and partly because you'd been jumping around for an entire football game. When I was In Control, you did this every Friday night. You plastered a smile on your overly made-up face and did what you had to.

The truth is, you hated cheerleading. You loathed every second of it. You hated the way you were treated; you hated how no matter how hard you tried, it was never good enough. You even hated the screaming from the crowd because you knew none of them were screaming for you. You wanted more then anything to just yell, "I quit!" and stomp off the blacktop track, your head held high. But you knew

I would never let you do that. I had complete Control. I made you stay. I lied to you, telling you this is what you should really want. You should want a life like the movies. How many would kill for blonde hair and a spot on a varsity cheerleading squad? I tortured you night and day with these questions, angry that you would put my happiness in jeopardy for your own sake. Then, I discovered that I was wrong. I was wrong in the worst way, and I never realized how badly I'd hurt you until it was too late. I kept your head in the clouds, expecting nothing to ever go wrong. I blinded you with false truths until it was too late. Until everything came crashing down. You lost everything with a single sentence. You fell farther then I thought possible. Everything was gone, and you were left with nothing but me. And then, I left you, too.

Before I went, I told you, you would never make it on your own. You would die like this. Alone, heartbroken, pathetic. I'll never know why you never listened. Maybe it's because you finally realized I was bad. That I was a liar and a cheat. That I had never really cared for you. It doesn't matter. What's important is that you took your life in your own hands for the first time. That was when I realized I would never get you back. That I had Lost Control.

Like a phoenix, rising from the ashes, you emerged a new person. Someone who didn't need a Controller. Gone were the voices telling you that you weren't good enough, that you couldn't make it. Gone was the skin stained orange with self-tanner. You painted your eyes dark as night because you thought black eyes were beautiful. Your hair became the color of fire, with only a few blonde roots remaining, the only evidence of who you used to be. You went by your name, your God-given name. Not the stupid, cutesy nickname I had insisted on before. You rediscovered your first, real, true love. She had been there since existence, waiting there just below the surface. You had pushed her away repeatedly in the past, but she finally forced her way to you. She taught you how to turn words into pictures, how to fall in love with a painting. She flowed from your hand onto countless pages of paper. You became obsessed with her, wanting to know everything you could. So you sit in a paint-splattered room for three hours a day, soaking up all you can of her. Breathing in her perfume of colors: red, yellow, orange, green, blue, purple, all of them. She saved you.

I don't know how to explain myself, my actions, to you. The truth is, I don't know why I treated you that way. She taught you to live. I had been teaching you to die. I had justified my actions by lying to you and myself. I know you forgave me long ago; the evidence is obvious. But, I can't give you back all the time you lost with me. During my Control you never had a chance. Guilt is my only emotion these days. Guilt for you, for me and for the fact that I can never change the past. I can't just apologize because that doesn't cover it. There's no

word in the English language that can express my remorse. All I can say is that I'm sorry. I'm sorry I was bad; I'm sorry you were good. I'm sorry I can't change it, and I'm sorry I can't fix it.

So here's to you, Nicole. I sincerely hope one day I can forgive myself as well. I swear, I'll never be In Control again. I love you.

Love, Nickie.

Sweet Oblivion

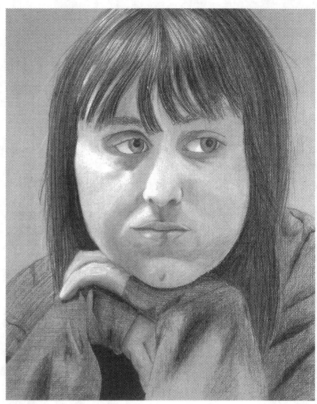

Poetry by Chantell Cooper, Freshman
Charcoal by Cheyenne McLachlan,
Sophomore

The sweet oblivion of sleep,
Eluding you each time you close your eyes.
Missing his soft, silky skin delicately stroking your cheek,
The trail of warmth refusing to leave your skin,
His hand no longer there.
His godlike face forever embedded in your mind,
The deep eyes that would bewilder you,
Freeze you in place,
Leave you befuddled from only glancing into them
For a single second.
Breath paused,
No longer able to think for yourself,
You are no longer in control of your own mind,
Your own body,
Your own heart.

Goodbye

Poetry by Chantell Cooper, Freshman
Oil by Brooke Poeppel, Senior

Love, simply described as the toying with one's heart,
With one's soul,
With one's mind,
With one's whole being,
The mind befuddled, leaving one speechless.
One cannot fight against the pain,
Cannot shield oneself against the insanity,
The pain,
The confusion,
The emptiness.
Let not one thought slip through such composure,
The temptation stronger than ever,
The want for things to be as they once were
For each day to pass with normalcy,
Both your mind and your heart at perfect ease.
The smile that brightened your face,
Lingered on your lips, once as a genuine smile
Now is forced upon your face,
Poorly done, coming out as a sneer, a grimace.
How you long for the sweet embrace,
The enchanting laugh,
The godlike smile of your, now secret, love.
The sweet memories haunt every inch of your mind,
Finally giving up the hope which has carried you thus far...
The final goodbye.

The Monster

Poetry by John Dolph, Senior
Charcoal by Nekodah Niedbalski, Senior

Across snowy plains I flee
from pursuit of my creator.
Each step I take
I take on borrowed legs.
Each breath that escapes by mouth,
pushing misty smoke before my face,
finds its way outside
by way of rotten lungs.
A heart inside me beats
to the desires of another man.
What is man?
Who am I?
From the peace of blackness
what passes as consciousness for me
was snatched
then pulled back,
back to the harassing sights and sounds
of these large and meaningless thoughts.
Yellow eyes take in a world
that holds no place for such as me.
I do not belong here.
I should be dead.
Across snowy plains I flee
from pursuit of my creator.
Each step I take,
each breath I pull,
each thought I think,
I gain by theft of life,
yet they are never mine.

Inside the Unseen Night and Outside the Jack-O'-Lantern

Poetry by Duane Williams, Senior
Charcoal by Garrett Blad, Sophomore

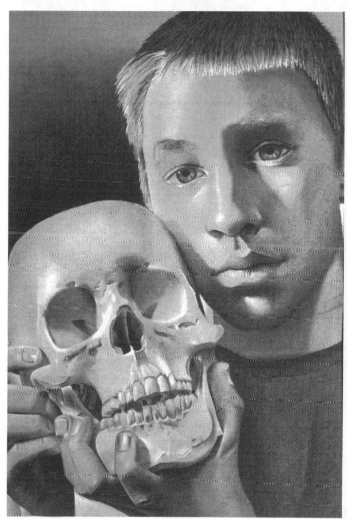

On the outside
I am the Avatar
Darkness incarnate
The blackness embodied
Within mortal coils
I am the unseen night
Starless and moonless
Uncaring in my feeling
Like the all-consuming
Black hole

On the inside
Melancholy is my name
Empty, like the jack-o'-lantern
Carved and hollowed
Flames burning within
Writhing and twisting
Only seen in the dark
By eyes unnoticed
Ignorant to the torture
Uncaring of the lost
The child of Babylon
Forever lost in Zion

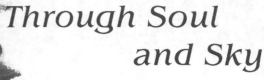

Through Soul and Sky

Poetry by Jacob Ladyga, Senior
Ink by Brooke Poeppel, Senior

A lonely soul looks to the sky
Eyes reflecting burning stars
With singing heart and burning tears
A rough-hewn path of love and fears
Bliss and peace soothe silent cries
Refreshing dew displaced with steps.

As the traveler meanders with light steps
Beneath the infinite stretch of sky
From where larks sing and utter cries
The One has hidden secret stars
In flowers, stones, and glistening tears
To guide us through the dark of fears.

Between choked gasps and passionate tears
As she took those tentative steps
Musing now on creeping fears
That seem so meek below the sky
And that wandering soul prayed on the stars
She uttered mild, mournful cries.

A lonely owl muttered her own cries
That briefly stopped the traveler's tears
She saw the two bright eyes, like stars
Moving on a branch with the creature's steps
Then with a rush, it took to the sky
A bird of prey, sans all fears.

Why couldn't she abandon fears
Release such triumphant and bold cries
And let her spirit take to the sky
Shedding no more melancholy tears
Taking soft transcendent steps
To the freedom of the stars?

The fading of nocturnal stars
As morning's warm rays dry her tears
Her journey's end, the ceasing steps
And retreat from the crippling cries
As light hits Nature's new fallen tears
Soft brightening across the sky.

The sweet embrace of sky and stars
Releasing all of her tears and fears
The traveler cries with wavering steps.

Someone, Please Ask Me

Poetry by Charly Porter, Senior
Pastel by Nekodah Niedbalski, Senior

I am quiet
For too many reasons
That no one seems to know about.
No one will ever know
For I fear
It'll be living inside me
For too many years,
Though I take breaths everyday
Hoping that eventually the pain will go away.
I hardly know myself anymore.
The girl I look at in the mirror
Appears as me,
But her insides are a wreck.
What will I do?
He thinks he didn't do anything wrong;
He'll get his pay back.
I feel like trash,
Just a waded up piece of paper.
No one will ever know.
It's my secret, but
Will someone please just ask me, what's wrong?

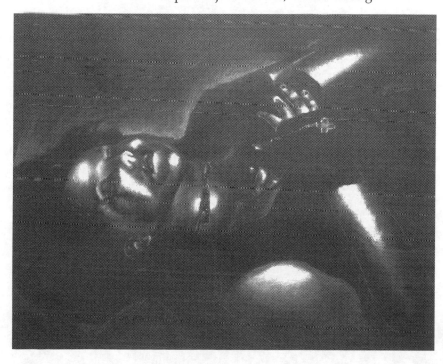

Awareness

Poetry by Nathan Stull, Senior

We all worship in different ways
But at the core it's all the same
A battle for truth in an ongoing game
In a world playing for nothing

They've yet to sell it in a store
Which makes us equal with the poor
Who sleep on history that is the floor
Of a world that's gaining nothing

Ajnya was placed for all to see
The point of life is only to be
But not until your mind's set free
Of a world that's caught in nothing

Get up, there's no more need to crawl
To seek sense in a pulsing wall
Energy that feels so raw
In a world that's teaching nothing

Find out who you really are
Rise to the sky and grab a star
They make it seem you must go far
Out of a world surrounding nothing

Be it magnet or God who's 10 feet tall
They've grown us keys so when we fall
We may grow larger or grow small
In a world reaching for nothing

After you see there's so much more
Newspaper taxies appear on the shore
Clouding your head with stories of war
In a world practicing nothing

Sometimes you must touch the ground
Re-tying ropes that make you bound
Silence broke by the sound
Of a world that's screaming nothing

They'll tell you not to come my way
My sacrament pulls all astray
By staying there you mold like clay
In a world leaving nothing

Generations that are being taught
To drink up fun within a shot
It's legal poison that isn't caught
In a world enforcing nothing

Enlightened is not up to par
Instead get dumb inside a bar
Then drive home in a cloud of noire
To a world that's sick from nothing

The choice to choose is whether to rot
And be judged on only what you've bought
Or fulfill a helpless life that's caught
In a world that feeds on nothing

I can only help you leave
It's up to you that you conceive
That this is your Incarnate's Eve
At least you'll purge with something

To Attack or Not to Attack
-A Tragic, Modern Soliloquy-

Poetry by Garrett Smith, Senior
Watercolor by Nathan Finley, Junior

Enter George W. Bush

GEORGE:

To attack or not to attack-that is the question:
Whether this war be right and I would suffer from the forums and
interviews of outrageous disapproval, or I could find justification even
when there is none, and by attacking, gain oil. To stay, to invade no more-
and by staying, we cut spending and save a thousand lives that need not
be consumed by the horrors of war. To stay, to remain peaceful: ay, there's
the problem, for if I invade, rewards may come when we have occupied
this simple country, and of this, I cannot help but think, and it gives me
pause. For others, the calamity of peace is pleasing. For who, but I, could
bear the whips and scorns of Time magazine, being the oppressor and his
wrongs, versus the pangs of doing Nothing with my delay? Who is it who
holds this office and the troubles from such a wrong and unlawful war? But
how can they possibly understand what weight I bare? Who would bear
my load other then Me, for I might grow weary from the bombardment
of disapproval? Then there's History to account and the dread of being
forgotten after death, those who have passed Never to return or be
remembered; it puzzles me still and makes me Attack with what ill
intentions I do have. Then the missiles shall fly onto the nation of Iraq,
for a conscience will make a coward of us all, and it is better to act now
and to get a resolution later. The people are pale in their thoughts, and my
bureaucratic friends of great pitch and power will accept this even as the
currents turn awry and my approval drops below 30%, for Bush is the name
of action.--Soft you now, the fair Laura! --Nymph, put me in your prayers,
for all my sins will be remembered.

A MENTAL Interaction

Drama by Nicole Noland, Senior
Scholastic Writing Awards Gold Key Winner - American Voice Nominee
Pen by Nicole Noland, Senior

SETTING: Inside the mind of 17 year old Nicole Noland, John Glenn High School student. A typically chaotic place, it is now almost completely empty. The mental version of herself is scurrying around, moving various things out of the way. She looks a bit stressed out, and keeps talking to herself: "You need to get started on that English paper. You need to start writing." She yanks open a door with a huge sign that says "SUBCONSCIOUS" and shoves random objects into it. As the door closes, we can see that she has also stuck Tim Burton, Holly Black, a blue-tinted faun and a taco in there.

Fall Out Boy's lead singer, Patrick Stump, enters. He strolls over with his guitar and his I LOVE BINGO trucker hat.

Patrick: Hey, sugar. I love you. Marry me.

Nicole: *looking up from a stack of art school papers* Not now. I don't have time to fantasize about you. I've got an English paper due tomorrow, and I need it to be empty in here.

Patrick: But I wrote this song for you, and we were going to play it at the Warped Tour! *clings to her leg*

Nicole: *shaking him off* Later. I'll think about you in Algebra class, okay? Go away.

Patrick: Humph. *stomps off into subconscious part of brain and slams the door*

Nicole: *sighing* Okay * picks up a clipboard* Okay, you guys. Let's get The Green Mile in here first, and we'll go from there.

The characters from the film The Green Mile all walk in. Several men in prison guard uniforms enter first, followed by prisoners in black and white striped jumpsuits.

Nicole * eyeing the prisoners' clothing* Wow, could you guys have possibly worn anything more cliché?*wrinkles nose* ...And you smell.

Edward Delacroix: Hey, cut me some slack. I was burned alive. I can't help it.

Nicole: Not you. Him. * points to Wild Bill Wharton, who is being wheeled in wearing a straightjacket and fighting to break out of it.*

Wild Bill * in a singsong voice* I currently got some tuuuuuuurds...

Everyone: SHUT UP!

Edward: They should have fried you. You got the easy way out. Look at me. * a chunk of charred and blackened skin falls off his head*

Percy Wetmore: I already apologized for that, you idiot.

Edward: Oh, and like you didn't know the electrocution sponge had to be wet?

Paul Edgecomb: Del, knock it off. Percy, shut up or we'll put you back in solitary.

Nicole: Okay, okay. Just line up together, and I'll organize you when everyone gets here. *looks around* Where's John?

Percy: He's with the other Stephen King Literary Good Guys. Why that man wrote me as such a jerk, I'll never know.

Paul: *distractedly* Because he needed clearly defined characters in the moral sense to coincide with a book written about death row.

Percy: *blinks* Whatever. I'll go get him. *exits*

Nicole: I want you guys to make room for the next group. Hamlet's coming in next.

Everyone else groans What's wrong?

Paul: Don't you think we've put up with your fan girl crap for long enough?

Nicole: *blushing* I don't know what you're talking about.

Trumpets blare loudly as King Claudius and Queen Gertrude enter. Claudius has a dagger still sticking out of his chest. He doesn't seem to notice it. Gertrude is holding a empty goblet in one hand. Her skin is a pale gray color. She coughs loudly for a minute

and spits a pearl into her palm.

Gertrude: *to Claudius* I'm still mad at you for poisoning me.

Claudius: Like I knew you were going to drink it. Anyway, your own son stabbed me!

Gertrude: Well, you made him mad. It serves you right.

Nicole: Hey.

Claudius: Oh, good Lord. You AGAIN?

Nicole: Why does everyone keep saying that? For your information, I need you all for

a paper I have to write.

Gertrude: Let me guess. It's in Mr. Hernandez's class.

Nicole: Yup.

Gertrude: Figures. He's had his students sticking us in all sorts of places for years. One kid put us on Jerry Springer. Like I would seriously go on Springer.

Claudius: Well, I mean, you DID marry your husband's brother...

Gertrude: SHUT UP! *she clocks him upside the head with her goblet, knocking him out cold.*

Nicole: So, about Hamlet...

Gertrude: Relax. He's here somewhere.

Hamlet, Prince of Denmark, the original emo kid, enters. He whistles shrilly, announcing his arrival and leaps on top of a table that magically appears.

Hamlet: Hey.

Nicole: *blushing again* Hi, Hammmm-let....*All characters groan loudly*

Nicole: You're so pretty. I like your hair.

Hamlet: *shaking side-swept bangs out of his face* Thanks. I wear my hair like this so everyone knows how sad and depressed I am. I also like to contemplate suicide.* raises fists into the air* To be…. or not to be?

Gertrude: Hamlet, honey, get down from there. We all know you're too busy hating me to kill yourself... *looks around* ...or avenge your father's death.

Hamlet: *puts his hands on his hips* Well, you're the tart that went off and married your brother-in-law.

Nicole: Guys…*trails off, not even bothering to finish the sentence* I need everyone to make room for the Greeks.

Suddenly, trumpets blare loudly again. A chorus of Greek men in togas prance simultaneously into view and begin to sing loudly and off key.

Chorus: Oedipus! Wasn't stumped by the riddle! Oedipus! Left on a mountain when he was little! Oedipus! He sure is the bomb! Oedipus! He had sex with his mom! And..Here..He…IS!! *begin clapping frantically* Oedipus enters, bowing gracefully. He, too, is wearing a toga and a crown on his head. In a loud, booming voice he announces:

Oedipus: Everything is under

control now! I'm here to take over!

Nicole: Thanks, but I think I can handle it.

Jocasta peeps out from behind him. She still has a noose hanging from around her neck.

Jocasta: Hi.

Everyone: Hi, Jocasta.

Jocasta: *tearfully* I can't take this! I hate my life! *spins around and runs back out*

Oedipus: *eyeballing Gertrude* Hey, Hamlet.

Hamlet: Yeah?

Oedipus: Isn't your mom hot?

Hamlet: Uh.....She's pretty....

Oedipus: But don't you think she's like, soooo sexy?

Hamlet * repulsed* No! She's my mom!

Oedipus: *blinks* So?

Paul: Of course that would come out of HIS mouth.

Edward: That's sick. *barfs into a bag*

Nicole: I can't even concentrate on why I even need you, frankly.

Oedipus: *proudly* You need me because you can't just use characters from movies to write your essay.

Nicole: Whatever dude. Freud might have come up with a theory using your name, but you are just outright nasty. You're outta here.

Oedipus disappears into thin air with a poof, along with his flamboyant chorus.

Gertrude: I feel violated

Paul: Don't we all?

Nicole: Okay, so I'm still missing a bunch of characters. I want to know exactly WHAT is taking Percy so long with John and...*looks in every direction* ...where is Ophelia?

There is a loud noise in the distance, sounding faintly like a girl's voice, singing shrilly. With that, Ophelia bursts into view, her arm linked with Mary Tyrone's. They both look disheveled and are gazing blankly. Ophelia is dripping wet, still holding bunches of now-dead flowers. Mary keeps playing with her hair, her arms covered in dark bruises.

Ophelia: *sings* He is dead and gone, lady...

Mary: The foghorn keeps me awake at night...

Ophelia: *singing again* Hey nonnie, nonnie, nonnie, hey!

Mary: ...That's why I'm always up.

Edward: Mary, everyone in here knows you're a morphine addict. You don't need to hide it.

Mary: *patting her hair* What do you mean? I don't know what you're talking about. It's my hair, isn't it? Something is wrong with my hair.

Jamie, Mary's eldest son, stumbles in, completely hammered.

Jamie: The mad scene! Enter Ophelia!

Paul: The real Ophelia is already here, nimrod.

Jamie: Huh? Where? *looks around* Oh. There you are.

Ophelia is now curled up in a corner, talking to herself in a high-pitched, sing-song voice. She is playing with a handful of twigs.

Ophelia: I've got these beautiful flowers for each of you. *hands a twig to Gertrude* I'd give you violets, but they all shriveled up and died with my father. *Spins

around in circles, singing again* Hey, nonnie nonnie nonnie, hey!"

Hamlet: Now there's something one doesn't see every day.

Gertrude: Hush. This is all your fault, anyway.

Hamlet: Whatever. I didn't hold her head underwater. She's obviously too needy and clingy, anyway. I can't stand girls like that.

Nicole *eagerly* I'm not needy! What about me? Huh, Hamlet? What about me?

Jamie *belches loudly* I'm as drunk as a fiddler's bitch. Hey, Mama. You still all drugged up?

Edward: That's not very nice.

Jamie: What? It's not like it isn't obvious. She's just got no willpower to quit.

Mary: That's not true. I don't know what you mean.

Nicole: Jamie, knock it off. Here.*hands him another bottle of whiskey, hoping this will make him pass out and shut up.*

Jamie: I luuuuuv you fat girls. *Downs bottle in one drink and promptly passes out* *Nicole rolls her eyes*

Nicole: All right guys, I'm just gonna cheat and only use one more character, instead of the entire character list of Owen Meany. So....

Paul: Fine, whatever. You're the one getting graded.

Hamlet: Yeah, but I bet she could make up for it if she did some long comparison of John Coffey and Owen Meany.

Nicole: You are so smart.

Edward hurls again.

Right on cue, Percy reenters, rolling his eyes.

Percy: He won't come in.

Nicole: What? I need him in here to finish this essay!

Percy: I don't know what to tell you. He said it's too dark.

Gertrude: *snorts* Imagine that. Nicole Noland's mind being dark.

Nicole: * to Gertrude* You shut up. I can make you sound a lot worse than I already have.

Hamlet: I don't get why it's still dark in here. I mean, she locked Anne Rice and Tim Burton up already.

Paul: Wow. Way to not stereotype there, Hammy.

Edward: Just drag him in here.

Percy exits and reenters, dragging an enormous African American man in overalls behind him. The man looks around nervously.

John: I's scared of the dark, ma'am.

Nicole: No, no. It's not dark. Look.

A huge nightlight magically appears

John: Okay....

Owen Meany marches in, holding an air of importance. He has no arms, only bloody stumps hanging from his shoulders. He is all of 5 feet tall with incredibly pale skin and is extremely skinny.

Owen: HELLO.

Edward: Hey Nicole! I think we finally found someone as short as you!

Nicole: Shut up, Del.

Owen: I WAS THINKING MAYBE YOU COULD WRITE ABOUT ME AND THE WHOLE DEBATE ABOUT THE COMPARISON TO JESUS. I MEAN, YOU HAVE TWO CHARACTERS WHO HAVE SIMULARITIES TO CHRIST. I BET IF YOU WROTE AN ESSAY ON IT, HE WOULD GIVE YOU AN "A."

John: *asking Paul* Is I supposed to be Jesus, too, Boss?

Paul: I think so.

Nicole: Owen, don't you think it's ironic how two different authors wrote a character to be a religious figure and they are complete opposites.

Owen: WHAT DO YOU MEAN, EXACTLY?

Nicole: Okay, well, look at you. You're tiny and high pitched. And white.

Hamlet: Oh, so now we're bringing race into this?

Gertrude: Kindly shut your face, darling heart. She doesn't have to be politically correct inside her head.

Nicole: ...and John is like, 7 feet tall and has this really deep voice. And he's black and afraid of everything.

John: I is not.

Everyone: You are, too.

John: *shrinks back* 'Kay.

Edward: Do you think Mr. Hernandez did it on purpose?

Gertrude: Did what on purpose?

Hamlet: Gave his class two different stories incorporating Jesus symbolism.

Paul: I'm not sure, really. My only real opinion is that A Long Day's Journey shouldn't have won a Pulitzer Prize .

Gertrude: *puts her hand on her hip* And why not?

Edward: I have to agree with Paul. I think it was just a recollection of a dysfunctional family. More like a diary entry then a novel, really.

Owen: BUT HE FICTIONALIZED IT, SO IT WAS A DRAMA LIKE A NOVEL.

Hamlet: I just can't stand Jamie.

Gertrude: Who can?

Everyone begins discussing Eugene O'Neil in detail

Nicole: Uh, guys? Guys, I need to get this essay started.

Hamlet: Ophelia is NOT the same character as Mary Tyrone! Take it back, Edward!

Edward: C'mon, Hammy. I mean, don't you think there's a few similarities?

Gertrude: He has a point...

Hamlet: *pulls out a sword* Say somethin' else 'bout my 'Philly, and I'ma cut yew.

Paul: Hamlet, you made her go crazy. Why would you care if someone insulted her?

Gertrude: Don't talk to my kid like that!

Hamlet: Shut up, tart!

Gertrude gasps out loud

Nicole: *wearily* Come on, guys....

Everyone ignores her, and begins to fight viciously. Ophelia and Mary sit in the corner, staring blankly ahead. Occasionally, Mary pats her hair. John is sitting in another corner, sucking his thumb. Owen is perched on a chair, watching with disgust.

Nicole: I give up. *pulls out a laptop covered in Fueled by Ramen stickers and begins to type* "Dear Mr. Hernandez. Sorry I didn't do my English essay, but I had a couple of issues..."

Joshua

Poetry by Josh Phillips, Senior
Pencil by Christian Merz, Freshman

Just a Juggalo, only a man, ever living, never dying.
On the wagons of life, a misshapen puzzle piece,
So sophisticated, so unpredictable, so emancipated, so impermeable.
He lives inside my head, so there's nowhere to hide.
Unknown to myself, a lost wraith, surrounded by green forests and weeds,
camouflaging me,
And I choke and stab and separate the feelings from me, until they're gone, like they
never belonged.

The Person I'd Like To Be

Poetry by Lisa Dammann, Senior
German Exchange Student
Tempera by Catrina Kroeger, Sophomore

What you see is me trying to act
Like the person I'd like to be.
I can't let go of who I am now.
You see, I care
About how you feel
And I listen to what you say,
Even though sometimes
I don't have the power to be there for only you.
When the leaves start falling,
Are you afraid they're going to knock you out?
When the sun slowly sets,
Are you afraid it might never rise again?
Who am I to take the burden from you?
I'm just a kid, you know.
I want to let go of all the leaves,
Grow new ones with a golden shine.
I want to turn off the light,
Stop glowing for a while
And then rise up so tall,
My old me can hardly reach.
For however many winters I may live,
Always shall I be there to take the burden
Of the unlived life.

Die Person, Die Ich Gerne Waere

Dichtung von Lisa Dammann, Deutsche Austauschuelerin
Translated into German by Eva Paulsteiner, Junior
German Exchange Student

Was du siehst, ist wie ich versuche, so zu handeln,
wie die Person, die ich gerne waere.
Ich kann nicht gehen lassen wer ich jetzt bin.
Du siehst, ich kuemmere mich
um deine Gefuehle,
und ich hoere mir alles an, was du sagst,
auch wenn ich manchmal
nicht die Kraft habe, nur fuer dich da zu sein.
Wenn die Blaetter anfangen, herabzufallen,
hast du Angst, dass sie dich ausser Gefecht setzen?
Wenn die Sonne langsam untergeht,
hast du Angst, dass sie nie wieder aufgehen koennte?

Wer bin ich, um dir die Last abzunehmen?
Ich bin nur ein Kind wie du weisst.
Ich will alle diese Blaetter gehen lassen,
es sollen neue wachsen,
mit einem goldenen Glanz.
Ich will das Licht ausschalten,
den Schein fuer eine Weile anhalten
und dann so hoch hinaufsteigen,
was mein altes Ich kaum erreichen kann.
Wieviele Winter ich auch leben moege,
ich werde immer da sein,
um die Last auf mich zu nehmen,
die Last des ungelebten Lebens.

WRONG Turn. Right Moment

Prose by Drew Vance, Senior
Pencil by Catrina Kroeger, Junior

He's sitting in the bleachers, wearing a bright orange and yellow band T-shirt with a pair of skinny black jeans on. His headphones are in his ears with his face looking down. All you see is his wild, black, green, and blue hair.

He is always near everyone else, but never engaging in conversation. He has a cute face with a distinct jaw line and smooth features. His eyes are icy blue with the longest eyelashes I've seen on a guy. Along with these features, he has three lip piercings: two on the left side and one on the right side. Everywhere he goes, the girls drool over him.

When he walks around, he is always listening to his iPod. Everyone assumes he is listening to the bands he wears on his clothes. He never takes the headphones out, and yet he manages to be one of the most brilliant students in our class. He reads constantly; I swear, it's a never ending process. His location is another unknown about him. No one knows where he lives, where he drives to, or who his parents are.

One day I turned down the wrong road, and it came to a dead end at the most beautiful house I have ever seen. It was surrounded by the prettiest woods and water sights. As I was turning around, I noticed this mystery man from school. He was outside under a tree with a book and his iPod. He noticed me and came running like I was an invader. I stopped the car and rolled down the window. He stared at me with those gorgeous blue eyes and this secret hiding in them. I explained my situation, and all he did was point straight, and then made a hand gesture to turn left at the stop sign. He never spoke. But as he was pointing, I did notice something in his hand. It was his iPod, and it revealed what he was listening to: "I'll Always Love You" by the group By Your Mother. That's when everything came full circle. That's the day I finally met Bryan Jones.

Travelers

Poetry by Ayla Felix, Sophomore
Photo by Hannah Hummel, Senior

Two travelers meet,
Their paths crossed by fate.
They stand and stare,
So unaccustomed to another face.
They smile and move,
One to his left, one to his right.
They laugh as they move back
And almost seem to dance,
Then one moves left
As does the other,
And they move past,
Walking farther down Fate's path.
Perchance their paths shall cross again
On one dewy morn'
Or one fading eve.
But till then they walk alone,
Traveling the path before them.

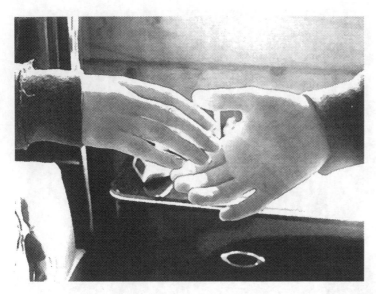

Hands

Poetry by DaLynn Clingenpeel, Junior
Photoshop by Hannah Hummel, Senior

Is this the girl those little feet follow?
The same person her parents look at with love?
Or is it just the same girl she pretends to be?
Her eyes reflect her soul,
Her true colors.
Lost and unsure about who she truly is,
She stares back at the person in the mirror.
Standing in the distance behind her
Are the smiling faces of her family,
But a second glance reflects their hurt
She contributed to causing.
With sad hopeful eyes,
They all stare back at her.
They're waiting.
Waiting for her to grow up.
Waiting for her to be the woman she was born to be.
Waiting for her to ask for help.
Their images blur as her eyes begin to tear.
Wiping away the shame,
Hands are gently placed on her back,
The hands that were always there to catch her
Every time she fell,
The hands that forgave her
Over and over,
The hands that are reaching out to help her again.

The Shy One

Prose by Kealie Petzke, Senior
Watercolor by Alysha Six, Senior

I have always been very shy. Over the years I've tried to become more outgoing, but in the end I'm still the same. Sadly, that's just the way I am. From my experiences, I've learned that if you don't speak up, you'll get eaten alive. In kindergarten that's exactly what happened.

My first few years of school seem so distant now. It's like there's a mist in my head, and no matter how hard I try to see, my vision fails me. Recently though, there was a break in the mist, and one memory was able to slip through.

Kindergarten was one of the worst years of my life. I didn't have any friends back then, which I blame mainly on my shy manner. The only friend I recall having was my teacher Mrs. Dodge, which I'm sure she wasn't aware of. Mrs. Dodge is one of the nicest people I've ever had the privilege of meeting. She tried very hard to get me out of my shell and to interact with the other kids.

One day I decided that I was going to try my hardest to play in the playhouse. The playhouse was the most popular toy in the classroom. Only four kids were allowed to play in it at a time, and it ended up being the same kids everyday. They were the cool kids at the time, and they always got "first

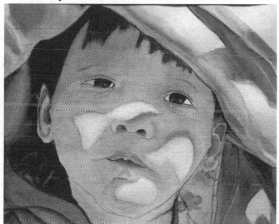

dibs" on all of the best toys. I had never gotten the chance to play in the playhouse before, and my dream was to be able to cook in the kitchen. Cooking consisted of plastic food in a plastic skillet on a plastic stove. Fake cooking was all the rage in kindergarten.

After building up enough courage to approach my fellow classmates, I walked up to them and asked in my sweetest voice if I could play in the kitchen for a little while. I saw the answer coming from a mile away. They just stuck their noses in the air and simply said, "No." At that moment my heart and my spirits were crushed. All I wanted to do was play in the playhouse. One minute in that kitchen would have made me the happiest and luckiest girl in the world, but those four kids took that away from me.

From then on I stopped trying to play with the other kids. Day in and day out, I sat by myself and played with all the leftover toys that none of the other kids wanted to play with. I felt like the dog being fed scraps.

Mrs. Dodge sent a note home to my mother one day. She expressed her concern for me because I seemed very sad and never played with the other kids. She was worried that something was going on, and she wanted to know if my mother knew of anything. I don't remember ever telling my mom about the things that went on at school. I was either too embarrassed or too sad to talk about it.

My mind just draws a blank after that. No amount of thinking gets me closer to remembering the rest of my kindergarten year. Maybe I simply forgot, or maybe I chose to forget because the memory of it was too painful. It's hard to say after so many years have gone by.

To this day I can't understand why those four kids acted the way they did. If I had been in their position, I would have let them play with me. I would have given them my spot in the kitchen and let them play with the plastic goodness. I wasn't in their position though, and I didn't get a chance to show them how nice I was. I was a shy, sweet girl, and because of that I got trampled on. I guess the saying is right: Nice guys finish last.

Do **Unto** Others...

Prose by Paige Weist, Senior
Tempera by Nicole Noland, Senior

My mother has worked at Martins for about eight years. There is a lady who works there named Sharon. Sharon is about 56 years old and is left raising her three granddaughters. The oldest one is Christine; she is about 14 years old. Christine's mother is in jail about every other week for doing something ridiculous.

One summer day Mom invited Sharon and her granddaughters over to go swimming. The night before, there was an incident, and the two youngest girls were taken away to live with their dad in California. Sharon wanted to get Christine out of the house so she could hopefully have some fun. I'd never met Christine before, and I was anxious to meet her. It was around 2:00 p.m. when they arrived. Christine was nothing like I expected her to be. She was tall and big boned. She was very quiet and shy; I tried my best to make her feel welcomed.

After spending the day together, I learned a lot about her. She is an outcast in the world. At school, no one includes her in activities because she doesn't look like her other classmates. Like I said, she's taller than the other kids, heavier, and her grandmother doesn't have a lot of extra money to spend on clothes. She is stuck with only so many outfits.

One day I took Christine shopping for her birthday. I got money out of the bank just to spend on her. We decided to go to the mall. She wanted me to help her find some clothes and shoes that were in style. I did my best to help her find something that would help her fit in a little better. While we were shopping, we saw two boys who went to school with her. They asked her what she was doing at the mall. Her response was that she was just shopping. One of the boys made a comment about "with what money." Christine's feelings were hurt; I could tell by the look in her eyes. I know what it's like to be very sensitive and emotional when it comes to what people think or say, because I am the same way. Right then and there I knew how she felt. We continued to shop. Christine found four new outfits, a few extra shirts and some shoes. I could tell that no matter what the boys had said, she was very happy with the outcome. After that day I've never heard her complain about the boys at school or anyone as a matter of fact.

After this experience, I learned that everyone just needs a friend. Whether it's to talk to or hangout with, we each just need someone there every now and then. I've never once judged Christine because of the way she's had to live her life. She's been through a lot: living with her grandma, seeing her mom doing drugs on the bathroom sink and going to jail, and watching her only half-sisters get taken away by their dad when she doesn't even know who her father is. I feel sorry for her and want to help her have a happy childhood as I once did. There isn't anything that I wouldn't do for her, because in a strange and different way, when I look into her eyes, I can also see myself.

Zero Blue

Poetry by Ethan Marosz, Senior
Watercolor by Allison Adkins, Junior

It's a dark, somewhat translucent shade
Like the color of water right before you drown,
Looking up at the world in which
        you used to live,
Thinking, "If only breathing had been
        this easy up there,,
I might have stayed around a day or two more."

It's the sky after you walk out of that hospital,
One acquaintance less and a few
        thousand conversations lost..
"If only they had held on," you say,
"I wouldn't have to sleep on this floor."

It's the color in her eyes
When there's nothing you can do
        to make her joyous,
And you think, "If I were better,
        she wouldn't ever
Have to face the same zero blue that I do."

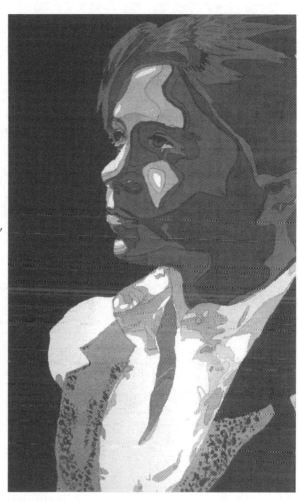

NO Clue AT ALL

Fiction by John Dolph, Senior

Photo by Kaleigh McMichael, Senior

There I sat in a small town ice cream shop, The Yum Yum Shoppe if you must know, listening to the clang of cooking utensils and the quiet murmur of the talking customers. The hot July sun was at its zenith and had driven a nice little crowd into the shop. I picked up little bits and pieces of conversation but honestly didn't care about the small town gossip and trivial small talk permeating through the shop. I had other stuff on my mind, other fish to fry you might say. There was a nun outside giving out free New Testament bibles. She had tried to shove one off on me when I came in. I had kindly refused.

As I sat in the higher than necessary stool at the end of the counter, my mind began to drift as it always does when I have nothing particularly interesting to do. While I was mulling over my thoughts and chewing on the end of my milkshake straw, I almost missed the woman I was looking for walking into the shop. I surely would have missed her, too, if not for the click of her high heeled shoes as she walked through the door. You're probably wondering why I was in that particular ice cream shop waiting for that particular woman to walk in, so I might as well take the time to explain the situation. I suppose I owe you at least that much. To make a short story even shorter, I'll give you just a brief summary of the back story to this whole ice cream shop tale. I'll give you enough to keep you interested but not too much as to bore you out of your mind. Fair? Good.

To begin with, I'll tell you that I'm a detective. I work for the state of Indiana and spend most of my time solving petty little cases that nobody, especially me, has any right to waste time on. For once though, I was actually put on a fairly important case. No longer a rookie on the force, I was finally up there with the big guys. I really don't know if you as a reader consider tracking down a female who had pulled off a couple of car thefts and armed robberies of small town banks and shops as high on your list of important activities, but hey, I was happy for the case, all right? At least, at first I was happy. Tracking someone for three months gets tiring and time consuming. By then I just wanted to catch her and get back to my nice, quiet desk at the station. Maybe I could even make one of my daughter's piano recitals. No, forget that. I hated them anyway.

According to my sources, that small shop in that small town was supposedly where she would pop up next. She had a knack for using elaborate disguises to pull off her heists, and I was to be on the lookout for some sort of wig and glasses that day. You can understand then that when I saw the woman with the glasses click her way into the shop, I became pretty excited. I was even more so when I saw how horrible the wig was. It was poorly made and hanging a little bit to the left. I was certain that meant she had no idea I was here and had her guard down.

I quickly turned the other way so she wouldn't see me watching. Waiting for the right opportunity, I continued to chew on my straw which was reduced to something that didn't even resemble a drink sipping device. I was so elated by the certain prospect of catching my quarry that the question of why she would be so sloppy didn't even cross my mind. I honestly didn't care either. She was there, and I was there, and I was finally going to cuff her.

As she made her way to an empty table, she was clearly visible in the shop keeper's mirror. I was going to use that looking glass to catch a real criminal that day, not someone dining and dashing on an ice cream bill. As the criminal proceeded to dig through her purse, I prepared to make my move. The shop door jingled again, signaling the entrance of another customer. It was the nun. The woman I was after was startled by the nun's entrance, and I realized that the nun had made the perfect distraction. I quickly rose and strode across the dining area toward her seat.

One problem though. As I bore down on my prey, the nun strode towards hers, which was me. Just before I had my badge out of my pocket, a long nailed finger poked itself into my chest.

"You, young man, need Jesus in your life," she said in a chortling voice, which was exactly how I always assumed nuns talked.

As I attempted to get around her black and white figure, I replied, "That might be so ma'am, but I'm a bit busy, so I think Jesus can wait."

"Heathen!" she screamed as I got around her. As I did so, she flung her stack of bibles at my back, knocking me off balance. Because I was in such a hurry, I took no notice

as I reached for the woman I would be arresting.

"Who do you think you are lady?" I shouted over my shoulder. As my hand pulled off the criminal's wig and my badge flashed out of my pocket, I heard an all too familiar voice call back to me.

"Not who you think I am officer!"

I took one look at the bald women I had just de-wigged and realized I had made a grave mistake. A thousand curse words ran through my mind as I felt the gun press against the small of my back and as I heard her voice tell me to drop my gun and give her my cuffs. Fearing for my life, I obliged. The nun, who was really the brown eyed criminal I was pursuing, then commenced to cuff me to the table that was occupied by the poor chemo patient I had just embarrassed. Everybody else in the room did as they were told and got down on the ground as she proceeded to rob the place blind. The entire time I just closed my eyes and kicked my mental self in the butt. I even let a little laugh escape my lips as she reached into my pocket and took my car keys.

I finally opened my eyes and looked into her chestnut colored eyes. She was beautiful; I couldn't lie. I suddenly had the strange urge to kiss her. She must have been reading my mind as she planted a big, wet one right on my lips.

"That was fun, Jeff. See you next time," she said. While walking out to my car, she looked back once over her shoulder, smiled, and playfully flipped her hair. I haven't seen her since.

My Inspiration

In Loving Memory of David Scott

Poetry by Emily Jaske, Junior
Colored Pencil by Nekodah Niedbalski, Senior

My life was good
happy, blessed, blissful,
and then I got the news-
news that was almost the same
as I got two years earlier.
Another person, friend, loved one
taken from me. Why does this happen?
Cancer - the word is only two syllables,
only takes a second to say,
but can cause a lifetime
of hurt, mourning, and tears.
That was how my life fell
apart because my golf trainer,
my second dad, my inspiration
was taken from me in a flash because of a two
syllable word that only takes a second to say.
How that word brings silence
and tears, nothing positive.
How I miss you, oh, how I miss you.

The Rest

Poetry by Heather Helminger, Senior

Watercolor by Nicole Noland, Senior

The sun hung low that day,
Another grave to fill.
We sat in silence and
The crows sang their sad song.
Too many souls have risen
Above this ground.
The ocean doesn't seem
Quite so inviting
Accompanied by the scent of the dead.
Land of the free, and here they lie.
Holy signs rest upon an unholy act.
When will this all cease?
The consumption of death is prominent.
Thick fog rests above my brother,
A blanket reassuring that one day he might
Come home.

Reflections of a Rear-view Mirror

Poetry by Jordan Lynch, Senior
Photo by Hannah Hummel, Senior

I've traveled many places
Though I see the same scene,
A teenage girl staring at me intensely
Trying to fix what she sees,
But I only tell the truth.

Friends in the back
Buckled safely,
Pictures snap while looking through me,
Hoping to turn out better,
But I only tell the truth.

He leans over to kiss her gently.
She looks up at me
With an indecisive expression,
But I can only tell her the truth.

Lights are always close behind.
She looks at me, and I show her
I can only tell the truth.

Many nights I'm left alone,
Forced to stare into the darkness.
I see nothing but the empty town streets,
And that's the truth.

Cold

Poetry by Emily Thomas, Sophomore
Pencil by Jessica Rose, Senior

The iron bells and the rain
In the distance a long black train
When the wind calls it says your name
On that day the sun drops
On that day the music stops
So I run away

The thunder and lightning ring
I wonder if you're listening
Your eyes are always shifting
Can you see me?
It's like you're not here
I claim it's my worst fear
So I run away

We'll dance inside this song
Of lovers who tried and have gone
But maybe I knew all along
That this heart would beat today
If only I know what to say
So I run away

Here I lie in the grass at your side
Never knowing what you clearly hide
The waves pick up and in comes the tide
Your body leans away from me
The fog clears and I now can see
That it was you who ran away

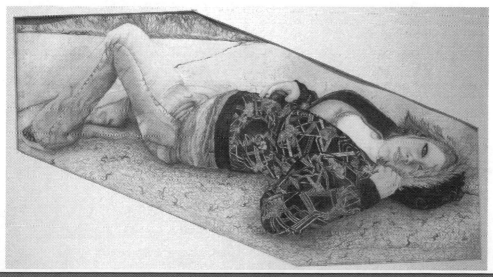

A Matter of Time

Poetry by Heather Helminger, Senior
Pencil by Heather Helminger, Senior

The rain fell down in angry
Waves while you stood in the
Doorway,
Faces sullen and masked from
The emotions at play.
The sky lit up every now and then,
Outlining the edges of your face.
The moment was embraced with
The presence of time.
Too many things were to blame,
At fault-
Lack of honesty, compassion, and
Understanding.
You needed to find your commitment,
Not waiting for your 'eventually.'
Actions speak louder than words,
A phrase that holds true.
Put aside
Feelings of regret and misconception,
Exile the feelings once felt, and I'll
Leave you with this empty house,
Along with my tattered being forever.
Walking away, drenched from the
Downpour, something will replace
This old habit.

Your Only Truth

Poetry by Kelsey Piotrowicz, Junior
Photo by Kayleigh McMichael, Senior

Everyday I hang on the wall to answer the questions you don't have to ask.
"What am I doing? Why did this happen?
What should I do? Where do I go from here?"
The answers are written on your face.
I'm here to tell you what you can't bring yourself to say.
I see the tears stained on your cheek,
The smile you get when you hear his name,
The guilt pouring from your expression,
The anger that seeps through your eyes.
I look at you, and you look back.
I don't see through; I see you.
The image isn't distorted.
No one else has to know.
It's only you and I, and I promise to judge you fairly.

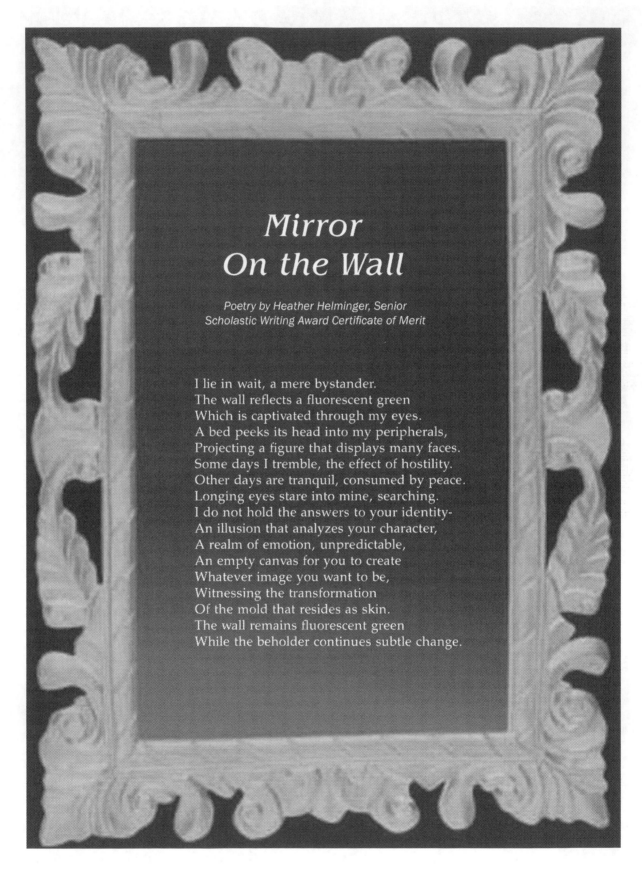

Mirror
On the Wall

Poetry by Heather Helminger, Senior
Scholastic Writing Award Certificate of Merit

I lie in wait, a mere bystander.
The wall reflects a fluorescent green
Which is captivated through my eyes.
A bed peeks its head into my peripherals,
Projecting a figure that displays many faces.
Some days I tremble, the effect of hostility.
Other days are tranquil, consumed by peace.
Longing eyes stare into mine, searching.
I do not hold the answers to your identity-
An illusion that analyzes your character,
A realm of emotion, unpredictable,
An empty canvas for you to create
Whatever image you want to be,
Witnessing the transformation
Of the mold that resides as skin.
The wall remains fluorescent green
While the beholder continues subtle change.

Contributors